WILDFLOWERS

OF

ARKANSAS

by Carl G. Hunter

The Ozark Society Foundation
Little Rock, Arkansas

OTHER SPONSORS

Arkansas Game and Fish Commission

Ross Foundation

Winthrop Rockefeller Foundation

Carl G. Hunter

Second Edition, 1988

Third Edition, 1992

Fourth Edition, 1995

Fifth Edition, 1999

Published by

The Ozark Society Foundation
Little Rock, Arkansas

Library of Congress Catalog Card Number: 88-92463
ISBN Number: 0-912456-16-7

THE OZARK SOCIETY FOUNDATION

The Ozark Society Foundation is a non-profit, tax-exempt organization dedicated to the enjoyment and preservation of the Ozark Region of the United States through educational projects and publishing activities.

Members of the Board of Directors are:

Bob Fisher, Chairman	Jonesboro
Harold Hedges, Treasurer	Harrison
Tom Foti	Little Rock
Tom McRae	Little Rock
Bob James	Little Rock
Neil Compton (Deceased)	Bentonville

To order books or for more information write:

The Ozark Society Foundation
P. 0. Box 3503
Little Rock, AR 72203

The Foundation wishes to pay tribute to the memory of the late Maxine Clark for her many and varied contributions to the understanding and knowledge of the wildflowers of Arkansas.

DEDICATION

To Dr. Dwight M. Moore, who knew the wildflowers of Arkansas so well and who taught so many others to know and appreciate them.

CONTENTS

WILDFLOWERS OF ARKANSAS

Cooperators

NORTHWEST ARKANSAS
Dr. Edwin B. Smith, University of Arkansas, Fayetteville
Dr. Dwight M. Moore, (Deceased),
Mrs. Dwight M. Moore, Rudy

NORTHEAST ARKANSAS
Ruth Wade, Cherokee Village

NORTH CENTRAL ARKANSAS
Edith Huey Bartholomew and Harry Bartholomew, Mountain View
Mike Cartwright, Game and Fish Commission, Fifty-Six

WESTERN ARKANSAS
Dr. Gary Tucker, FTN Associates LTD, Little Rock
Aileen McWilliam, Mena (Deceased)
Lana Cook Ewing and Bruce Ewing, Mena
Gwen Barber, Mulberry

CENTRAL ARKANSAS
Bill Shepherd, Natural Heritage Commission, Little Rock
Dr. Jewel Moore, University of Central Arkansas, Conway
Jim Ettman, Jim Ettman Enterprises, Morrilton
Randy Johnson, Pinnacle Mountain State Park
Steve N. Wilson, Game and Fish Commission, Little Rock

SOUTHWEST ARKANSAS
Dr. Daniel England, Southern Arkansas University, Magnolia
Dr. Gerald Teasley, Texarkana
Ray Erickson, Soil Conservation Service, Lewisville

SOUTH ARKANSAS
Carl Amason, Calion

SOUTHEAST ARKANSAS
Edwin Gregory, Parkdale, (Deceased)
Marie Locke, Pine Bluff (Deceased)
Dr. Howard Stern and
Jane Stern (Deceased), Pine Bluff

CROWLEY'S RIDGE
Larry Lowman, Ridgecrest Nursery, Wynne

GRAND PRAIRIE
Sophia McCoy, Stuttgart (Deceased)

ACKNOWLEDGMENTS

The author is grateful to many persons who helped with the various phases of locating and photographing the wildflowers of Arkansas; also to those who helped in the preparation of the text and the descriptions of the flowers and plants. The material was reviewed by several persons who edited it and made comments which helped to improve the accuracy and readability. These people, who are listed on their own title page as COOPERATORS, have aided in putting this publication together. Their continued leadership, support, and assistance will be valuable to all who are interested in Arkansas' wildflowers.

Dr. Dwight M. Moore was the instigator of the project in 1977. This was certainly not a new role for him in this field.

Dr. Gary Tucker, FTN Associates LTD, Little Rock, gave continual guidance, assistance. and encouragement during the five year period required to complete the photography and the manuscript for "Wildflowers of Arkansas," including a review of all of the species descriptions for accuracy and consistency. He prepared the chapters entitled HISTORY OF BOTANICAL INVESTIGATIONS and FAMILY DESCRIPTIONS. The first describes the work of early botanists and explorers in the state. The chapters of family descriptions were written especially for this publication and the descriptions treat the species that occur in Arkansas. This should be especially useful to those who are interested in the flora of our state.

Bill Shepherd, Dr. Jewel Moore, the late Aileen McWilliam and Jeff Rettig reviewed introductory chapters and species descriptions. Dr. Edwin Smith reviewed the section on Composites. Jim Ettman reviewed all of the material pertaining to the Orchid Family. Dr. Smith and Dr. Tucker gave needed help with identification of species. Dr. Carl Slaughter provided the updated name changes in the Orchid Family.

Bill Shepherd and Edith Huey were especially helpful in locating many species in the field.

David Hunter shared his valuable knowledge of photography. Bruce Cook and Kerry Kemp provided lettering for the various drawings and the state map of physiographic regions.

Scott Hunter of Correct Color, Little Rock, was the printing consultant. He took the original film, supplied by Magna IV, and converted it back into a digital format. He then made the color corrections and supplied final film.

Most of the photographs were taken by the author. Credit to those who supplied the additional photographs is given in the PHOTOGRAPHERS section. Without a cooperative effort it would have been difficult or impossible to assemble all of the illustrations within a reasonable period of time.

The author wishes to express his sincere appreciation to the Ozark Society Foundation for making possible the opportunity to print "Wildflowers of Arkansas."

Julie Hudson's help was essential in manuscript work and in typing all of the material for publication.

Printer, Consultant	- Correct Color
Color	- Correct Color
Design, Page Layouts	- The Watkins Company
Lithographed by Quebecor/Sayers	

FOREWORD

Most of the states surrounding Arkansas have had books covering wildflowers on a statewide basis for some time. Two sections of Arkansas have been represented by Edith Huey of Mountain View and Ruth Wade of Cherokee Village. Mrs. Huey has published "Ozark Wildflowers" I, II and III. Mrs. Wade has published "Arkansas Wildflowers". Dr. Carl Slaughter, Morrilton, produced "Wild Orchids of Arkansas" in 1993.

The present publication, "Wildflowers of Arkansas," is intended to include a comprehensive cross section of the wildflowers from over the entire state. Several botanists who have worked in Arkansas could have assembled and published a collection of photographs and descriptions for a thorough treatment of the wildflowers of the state, but for one reason or another the opportunity did not become available.

Introduction

INTRODUCTION

All of the wildflowers pictured and described in this book now grow or have grown within the boundaries the state. Most of them also can be found in bordering states or over large sections of United States.

A total of 488 flowers is presented by color photographs. In addition, 116 other flowers are described so that a total of 604 species of wildflowers is covered in this publication. A total of 80 families is included. It is felt that this provides a thorough representation of all of the major groups of wildflowers that occur in Arkansas. This state has a wide and beautiful variety of wildflowers because of the several types of terrain, soils and habitats.

HISTORY OF BOTANICAL INVESTIGATIONS

Numerous explorers made observations on the plants of Arkansas prior to settlement. Many of the earliest explorers made few comments on the plants of what is now Arkansas, but several made significant observations. Among the more noteworthy of the early visitors were Freeman and Custis (on an expedition on the Red River into southwest Arkansas in 1806), Bradbury (primarily in the Ozarks in 1809-11), Schoolcraft (primarily in the uplands in 1818-19), and Nuttall (1819). Nuttall's *Journal of Travels into Arkansas Territory During the Year 1819* is a classic, provides keen insight into the plants of the area, and should be read by all interested in the natural history of the state. Featherstonehaugh (1834) made observations on both plants and geological features over a large area of the state. The botanist Lesquereux studied both the fossil and living plants of the state in 1859. None of these workers were resident in the state.

Francis L. Harvey, teacher at what is now the University of Arkansas at Fayetteville, was the first professional botanist to live in the state for any period of time. Harvey studied Arkansas plants during the period of 1875-1885, at which time he moved to Maine.

The first comprehensive checklist of Arkansas plants was published by Branner and Coville in 1891. The Branner and Coville study was augmented by a publication of Buchholz and Palmer in 1926. Buchholz was a botanist at the University of Arkansas, while Palmer was employed by Harvard University; both made extensive collections and observations over the state.

The most significant workers in more recent times have been Delzie Demaree and Dwight Moore. Demaree and Moore both came to Arkansas to teach in the early 1920's and have been active until recently. Both taught in several Arkansas colleges and universities, made extensive collections, and published numerous papers recording their observations.

STATUS OF WILDFLOWERS

The areas in which wildflowers grow are in a constant state of change. In some cases these changes benefit certain flowers. Species that have been absent for years may reappear. Clear cutting of timber and disturbance of the soil for roadways or pipelines may encourage certain wildflowers.

Unfortunately, many practices such as chemical application, grazing and intensive farming have eliminated flowers and limited others in many sections to the relatively few protected spots where they somehow survive. Often the best locations for the wildflowers that remain are along the roadsides and railroads since this land is not subject to the same type of usage as the adjacent cultivated fields, pastures and hay fields. Vacant lots and other idle land around the edges of towns and cities sometimes support a surprising variety of wildflowers. Fortunately only a small percentage of the wildflowers is limited to wild and secluded sites. In most areas a drive along rural roads will reveal many of the species that occur in the locality. State and National Parks and Forests, Wildlife Management Areas of the Game and Fish Commission, and other such areas that protect the forest and ground cover contain species not easily found elsewhere. The Natural Heritage Commission has acquired natural areas that preserve wildflowers.

Many of the wild plants can be grown from seed, roots or cuttings. For some species, digging and replanting is not detrimental where these are species that are commonly found or that re-establish themselves readily. So much harm has been done, however, by unknowing persons who have picked or dug up the valuable wildflowers that this is not encouraged without the help of knowledgeable persons to assist and provide positive identification. It is very seldom, if ever, that we have done the flower a service by taking it from the wild.

Through various means immigrant flowers have become established. Some have attractive blooms that add to the beauty of our plant life.

ENDANGERED SPECIES

The Arkansas Natural Heritage Commission (ANHC) has as one of its responsibilities the keeping of records on rare plants in the state. Plants under consideration for threatened or endangered species listing by the U.S. Fish & Wildlife Service are monitored for location and status by the ANHC. These data have a bearing upon preservation programs for these species and other natural flora including the selection of areas for acquisition or other measures to perpetuate this segment of our heritage.

Because of the widespread nature of this endeavor, a cooperative effort between all of the various outdoor groups and individuals is needed. Information pertaining to rare wildflowers and plants may be obtained by contacting the office of the Arkansas Natural Heritage Commission in Little Rock.

PURPOSE OF THIS BOOK

There has been a long standing need to publish a comprehensive collection of photographs and general descriptions of Arkansas wildflowers.

The botanist, and also the student and advanced amateur, can use the various manuals and technical publications to identify wildflowers. Now, it is hoped that with this book the majority of those who are interested in wildflowers can either identify or put into the right family or genus almost any of the species found in Arkansas by comparing the plant with the photographs and descriptions found herein. It was intended also that this collection of photographs could serve as a text or companion to other publications for a visual reference to the shapes and colors of the plants and flowers.

There are so many similar species in some families and genera that only a cross section of some of these groups could be included. For instance, there are nearly 300 species of the Sunflower Family now listed for the state. For identification of many species technical procedures are necessary.

Botanical terms have been used only where necessary to distinguish between similar species. Where the species is distinctive and the picture clearly identifies it, general descriptions are given. Some species that are not illustrated have been mentioned to make the book a more complete treatment of Arkansas' wildflowers.

Most of the plants that are commonly seen throughout the state bear flowers or blooms at one time or another. With many of these plants the flower is not attractive or noticeable. There are a number of species of flowering trees, shrubs and vines with beautiful flowers and this could be the basis for a worthwhile publication. None of the tree species have been included in this book. Some of the vine and shrub species are shown.

In most cases, small flowers less than a quarter of an inch in size have not been included.

3

Some of these are very attractive when seen close up or magnified. This publication involves mainly the showy herbaceous flowers of sufficient color and size to attract our attention. Fortunately, in Arkansas, there is a large number of these for us to enjoy.

Although wildflower species have been used for food and medicinal purposes and are still being used to some extent in this way, there are dangers associated with these uses. Identification must be certain. The manner of preparation is often exacting. None of these uses are recommended or encouraged in this publication. There are publications by knowledgeable people on these uses of wildflowers. (See the REFERENCES section in the back part of this book.)

Becoming familiar with a group of plants such as the wildflowers, trees, shrubs, vines, grasses, etc., is an aid in recognizing and evaluating habitats or environments for various purposes including wildlife management. Use of the wildflowers for these purposes is practical because they are widespread and fairly easily recognized. Use of wildflowers by game species of wildlife is indicated in the text.

HOW TO USE "WILDFLOWERS OF ARKANSAS"

Those features of the wildflowers which best describe them and serve to help locate and identify them are included, such as the naming or taxonomy of the plant, description and size, habitat, distribution and time of bloom. Other facts of interest such as growth characteristics, use and origins of species are included for some flowers. But the primary purpose, above all else, is to show as naturally and truly as possible the color and form of Arkansas wildflower blossoms for the enjoyment of all who are interested enough to look through this book. It is hoped that many will become interested in trying to locate, identify and enjoy the wildflowers first hand - in the outdoors.

In this book the families of flowers are arranged in botanical or taxonomic order and the genera and species in alphabetical order by scientific name within the family. Botanists list the plants in order beginning with the simple or primitive ones and progressing to the more advanced species. This is done within two large groups: the monocotyledons (one seed leaf) and the dicotyledons (two seed leaves).

The species, genus and family groups are determined by similarity of flower and fruit parts and their arrangement. Two closely related species within the same genus may have very different growth characteristics and appear to the inexperienced observer to have no features in common. One might be a creeping vine and the other a tall, erect plant, but if the flower and fruiting characteristics are similar, the two plants could be closely related species and have the same generic (genus) or first name.

When one becomes even generally familiar with some of the main family characteristics, an order to the plants becomes apparent. Several families have similar keys to identification and their relationships can be seen. Some have unique features that easily separate them from the others. Many of the families have been a source of cultivated flowers and vegetables and bear the same names as these. Becoming familiar with the major families does not require a great deal of study but aids greatly in locating the section of the book wherein a species in question is described.

PLANT NAMES

Common Names

Nearly all plants have been given common names based upon the shape and color of the flower, the design of the leaves or other descriptive features. Many of the wildflowers in this country were given common names by early travelers and settlers who named them after similar flowers in their countries or after some resemblance to objects, animals, etc. with which they were familiar. Sometimes the use of the plant supplied a common name. Some examples of common descriptive names are: lizard's tail, cotton weed, buttercup, sunflower, blood root, Dutchman's breeches, goat's beard, orchid, violet, Indian potato, wild carrot, mint and quinine.

Several different flowers have been given the same common name. There are four or five 'blazing-stars.' Several are called 'coneflower.' A flower often has different common names in different localities. The Wild Carrot is also called Queen Anne's Lace or Bird Nest Plant. This results in confusion when discussing flowers and other plants. Therefore, the botanical or scientific name is the one used by those who study plants in order to achieve consistency in identifying and discussing them.

Botanical or Scientific Names

Latin and Latinized words from other languages are used to make up the two name (binomial) system. The first word or name indicates the genus to which the plant belongs. The genus is a group of very closely related plants. The second name is the species name for an individual plant within the genus. A plant family is made up of several genera (plural of genus). The family has a single name.

These names are descriptive in many cases, as are the common names. No two plants will have the same botanical name, however, and this is the most important difference in the two systems of naming plants. Some examples of botanical names which include descriptive Latin words for people, places and objects are as follows:

Claytonia virginica Named after John Clayton, an early American botanist. Also after the State of Virginia. Many plants were first discovered in Virginia or other states and so bear this type second or species name. This is the Spring Beauty.

Nymphaea odorata *Nymphaea* for nymph or water spirit and *odorata* for odor or fragrance. This is the white water lily.

Viola lanceolata *Viola* for violet and *lanceolata* for the lance-shaped leaves. This has the common name of Lance-leaved Violet.

Other botanical names are more complicated and difficult to translate. Sometimes there is disagreement among the authorities over the exact translation. The plant name is not complete unless a third name is added which identifies the authority responsible for naming the plant, thus: Penstenion laxiflorus Pennell.

In this publication the scientific and common names are based upon those used by Dr. Edwin B. Smith in his atlas entitled An Atlas and Annotated List of the Vascular Plants of Arkansas. His work should be consulted for the name of the authority.

DESCRIPTION

Several of the wildflowers have variations in the color of the bloom. This is most common in the white, pink, and blue or purple flowers. Differences in shading and color patterns of the blossoms are also found within a species. Hybridization greatly affects color patterns. For these reasons the coloring is described.

The descriptions include information on the arrangement of the flowers and leaves and other vegetative parts of the plant. In some cases the uses that have been made of the plants are of interest. Flowers have been introduced into this country, either by accident or intentionally. Where these have become established over a wide territory so that they are regularly found, they are considered a part of our wildflower flora and are included in this book. Alien species are noted.

Because the color photographs usually highlight the blossoms or show them close up so that they can be more readily identified and better appreciated by the casual observer, it is often difficult to get a perspective of their size. For this reason, the size of the flower and the size of the plant are usually given. In addition to measurements in inches and fractions of inches, the dimensions in centimeters (cm) and millimeters (mm) are also given. For large plants meters are used.

PHYSIOGRAPHIC REGIONS OF ARKANSAS

A meter is slightly over one yard in length.

A foot equals approximately 30 centimeters.

One inch equals approximately 25 millimeters or 2.5 centimeters.

Metric measurements are coming into more common usage and so are included.

One advantage of the metric system is that the measurements are in multiples of ten. A meter (slightly over one yard) contains 100 centimeters (cm) and 1000 millimeters (mm).

The size of the plant will vary considerably on different soil types and on different sites depending upon soil fertility, the ph (relative acidity or alkalinity), moisture and other factors. Some plants are very adaptable and adjust to a wide variety of conditions. Under the most favorable conditions the plants and flowers will reach their maximum size and beauty.

HABITAT

Habitat relates to the location or the surroundings in which the flower is found. This includes soil and moisture conditions and also the land use, surrounding vegetation, amount of sunlight and other factors. Flowers of a particular region are most often found along roadsides, railroads, streamsides, idle fields, cemeteries, bluffs and other places where there is less grazing or cultivation of the land. Some are limited to very restricted habitats that are in danger of being eliminated.

DISTRIBUTION

Distribution describes the area or areas within the state where the flower occurs. Dr. Edwin B. Smith of the University of Arkansas has compiled the localities for Arkansas plants as derived from collections of many other workers. Dr. Smith's book entitled An Atlas and Annotated List of the Vascular Plants of Arkansas currently summarizes the species locations by counties. Those interested in wildflowers can be helpful in this effort by advising Dr. Smith of any new county locations in which the various flowers are found. This Atlas provided the basic source of information on the distribution of wildflowers. In addition, location data were obtained from records of the Natural Heritage Commission and from various individuals in addition to the field work conducted by the author during the five year period of the project.

Regions of the State

The state is divided into four distinct physiographic regions: the Ozark Mountains, the Ouachita Mountains, the West Gulf Coastal Plain and the Mississippi Alluvial Plain, commonly known as the Delta. Within the Delta Region lie Crowley's Ridge and the Grand Prairie, which have unique features in relation to the state's wildflowers.

For the purpose of this publication the main features of these regions that affect the distribution of plants are the elevations, the topography or lay of the land, drainage, land use, and most importantly, the soils. There are minor differences in climate and rainfall.

The Ozark Mountain Region

The Ozarks have elevations of 250 to 2,400 feet above sea level. Approximately 20 per cent of the region is over 1,500 feet.

Parts of the region are rugged with long, deep valleys, sharp cliffs and ledges or benches. In the very northwestern part of the region and in scattered locations elsewhere are gently rolling lands referred to as prairies.

The principal rock formations are sandstone, shale and limestones. The soils are residual. They were formed from bedrock and have remained where they originated. Limestone soils are quite fertile and support a variety of interesting wildflower species.

The Ouachita Mountain Region

The Ouachita Mountains, unlike the Ozarks, were in remote ages subjected to intensive structural movements. The beds of rock were warped, twisted and folded. Elevations range up to 2,900 feet above sea level.

Mountains and ridges often run east and west and occur in groups. Principal rock formations are sandstones, shales and novaculites. Most of the soils belong to the sandy loam group. Except in the river bottoms, the soils are relatively thin. Many of the same flower species found in the Ozarks occur here, however, there is not the variety nor the abundance of wildflowers that can be seen in the limestone soils of the Ozark Region.

The Ouachita Mountain Region includes the Arkansas River Valley.

The West Gulf Coastal Plain Region

The Gulf Coastal Plain, like the Delta, was once covered by the Gulf of Mexico. Level and rolling lands, hilly sections, numerous bottoms and occasional prairies are found in the Coastal Plain Region. Elevations run from 59 feet - the lowest in the State - to about 700 feet.

The ancient Gulf of Mexico left deep beds of limestone, marl, chalk, sandstone and shale. In later ages, clay, gravel and silt were washed down from the Ouachita Mountains and covered parts of the old sea floor. Naturally, many of the soils are sandy, but clay and silt soils also occur.

The Mississippi Alluvial Plain or Delta Region

All of Eastern Arkansas is included in the Delta Region. The Delta is a part of the gulf coastal plain which the Mississippi River and its tributaries reworked.

Most of the region is flat. Elevations average only 100-300 feet above sea level. The alluvium deposited by the Arkansas and Mississippi Rivers is highly fertile soil. The Delta is the richest agricultural area in Arkansas. Although there are some wildflower species unique to this region, a greater variety is found in the other regions which speaks well for the wildflower's thriftiness insofar as soil fertility is concerned.

That part of Crowley's Ridge within Arkansas runs for a distance of 200 miles from southern Missouri to the Mississippi River at Helena, The Ridge is from one-half mile to twelve miles wide. At its highest point it is 550 feet above sea level. In soil and general elevation the Ridge corresponds to the bluffs along the east bank of the Mississippi River. Thousands of years ago the region was a plain, considerably higher than Crowley's Ridge today. The Mississippi, then in its youthful stage, cut out two troughs, leaving Crowley's Ridge as an isolated remnant of the old plain.

Crowley's Ridge has soils that are older than the surrounding alluvium including loessial soils which are an unusual feature. This soil is subject to severe erosion. Certain plants that occur on Crowley's Ridge are found nowhere else in the state. Others that occur correspond more closely to the flora of the Ozark Region than to that of the Delta Region.

The Grand Prairie lies west of the White River and southwest of Crowley's Ridge. It has terrace soils from alluvium older than that in the adjacent bottoms. The subsoil is compact and holds water on the surface.

There are no basic rock deposits exposed in the Delta Region.

TIME OF BLOOM

The main blooming period for each flower is indicated. This period varies from year to year depending upon temperatures, moisture conditions and the changing of the seasons. An early or late spring can vary the beginning of the blooming season for spring flowers as much as two to three weeks. Also, there is approximately ten days to two weeks difference in the time of bloom between the southern and northern parts of the state.

Some plants have very long periods of bloom. Fire and other factors can change this period. Mowing may cause a plant to put up late growth and bloom long after the normal period. Some flowers continue to bloom until frost kills the entire plant. The date of the killing frost can vary from year to year.

Because of these factors the time of bloom given for each flower can only be approximate.

Plates and Texts

Family Descriptions

Monocotyledons

(Monocots)

Plants with one seed leaf (cotyledon). The flower parts are usually in threes or multiples of three. The leaves usually have parallel veins.

Thirteen families of plants are treated here. These include most of the showy herbaceous wildflowers of the Monocotyledon group in Arkansas.

Families of Monocotyledons not treated include the grasses, sedges, rushes, duckweeds, pondweeds, bur-reeds and other small-flowered plants.

Except for two of the Day-flowers *(Commelina),* all of Arkansas' monocots are perennial species.

FAMILY DESCRIPTIONS

MONOCOTYLEDONS

Water-plantain Family   *Alismaceae*

Herbs of aquatic and semiaquatic habitats, often with arrowhead- shaped leaves, with flowers having 3 green sepals, 3 white petals, numerous stamens and usually numerous pistils. About 10 taxa in the family in Arkansas. Members of the family sometimes are cultivated in fishponds and water gardens for their attractive flowers and foliage. Several members of the family provide tubers and spongy leaf and stem tissue as food items for various types of water birds and wildlife.

Palm Family   *Palmaceae*

Trees or shrubs (shrubs only in Arkansas) with unbranched trunks, large fan-shaped compound leaves with sheathing bases, and a conspicuous branched panicle of small flowers. A single native species, *Sabal minor,* in the family in Arkansas. Numerous cultivated species of horticultural or economic value belong to this family; the cultivated coconut of commerce is an example.

Arum Family   *Araceae*

Herbaceous plants, typically of moist or wet places, with often pinnately veined leaves. Individual flowers are tiny and insignificant but are associated with the spathe and spadix, which are characteristic for this family. The fruit is a fleshy berry and often red or orange in color. Many members of this family are poisonous, and no member of the family should be eaten unless identification is absolutely certain. The so-called Indian turnip or Jack-in-the-pulpit, *Arisaema atrorubens*, often is the subject of horseplay on the part of children; rootstocks and other parts of the plant are strong irritants to the delicate linings of the mouth and throat and should not be given to anyone as a joke. Cultivated members of the family include Monstera, Philodendron, Calla lily, and Dieffenbachia. Four taxa of the family grow wild in Arkansas.

Yellow-eyed grass Family   *Xyridaceae*

Rushlike plants with narrow leaves having sheathing bases, bases often pinkish in color. Flowers have a rather complex structure but are characterized by 3 showy petals, almost always yellow in color. Flowers in a single compact head that terminates each stem; only a few flowers will be open at any one time and the individual flowers are very short-lived. About 5 taxa in the family in Arkansas, almost always growing in wet places.

Pineapple Family   *Bromeliaceae*

Represented as a native plant in Arkansas by a single species, *Tillandsia usneoides* (Spanish Moss). This single species does not give a complete view of the diversity within the family. The more common representatives of the family are epiphytic or terrestrial herbs with rosettes of leaves that often are spiny, and with brightly colored flowers in conspicuous inflorescences having brightly colored bracts. Individual flowers typically have 3 sepals and 3 petals. Cultivated pineapple and numerous "bromeliads" in cultivation belong to this family. The brightly colored bromeliads are often seen in florist shops, conservatories, and grocery store plant departments.

Pipewort Family   *Eriocaulaceae*

Herbs of aquatic or serniaquatic habitats, stemless or short-stemmed, with a cluster of narrow grasslike leaves, and a tuft of fibrous roots. A dense head of very small flowers terminates the leafless flower stalks. The flower heads usually are white or gray in color. Only two species of the family occur in Arkansas. Members of the family are of little if any economic significance, and they are doubtfully of any significance as wildlife food plants.

Day-flower Family   *Commelinaceae*

Annual or perennial herbs with succulent, usually mucilaginous stems (seen when broken), leaves alternate, entire, and with prominently closed leaf sheaths, flowers with 3 green sepals, 3 petals usually colored either pink, blue, or purple, and 6 stamens having markedly hairy filaments. Flowers are almost always associated with a showy bract, the spathe. Leaves and stems often have a considerable amount of purple or purplish coloration on them. Approximately 14 members of the family occur outside cultivation in Arkansas. A number of members of the family are cultivated for their showy flowers and easy-to-grow foliage. The various types of Wandering Jew, Moses-in-the-cradle, and Spiderwort are commonly cultivated members of the family.

Pickerel-weed Family   *Pontederiaceae*
Herbs of aquatic and sermaquatic habitats with more or less irregular flowers from a spathe. Flowers have 6 perianth parts that are colored alike (often blue or pink), and there are 3-6 stamens. Leaves characteristically are long-petioled. About five members of the family occur in Arkansas. The most well-known member of the family probably is Water-hyacinth, *Eichhornia crassipes,* a beautiful but noxious plant that has invaded waterways of the South, making for serious navigational problems.

Lily Family   *Liliaceae*
Herbs with bulbs, rhizomes, corms, or tubers. Leaves often alternate, simple, often linear, and with parallel venation. Flowers with 3 petallike sepals, 3 petals, 6 stamens,and a pistil of 3 united carpels; ovary superior; fruit a capsule or a berry with numerous seeds. Flowers usually are showy and brightly colored. The family is represented in Arkansas by approximately 55 taxa. The family is a source of many ornamentals and a few species having medicinal properties. Some of the best-known cultivated members are Tulip, Hyacinth, Lily-of-the-valley, and Asparagus.

Amaryllis Family   *Amaryllidaceae*
Perennial herbs from a bulbous rootstock, sometimes from a rhizome. Leaves alternate, simple, usually more or less strap-shaped, usually few and basal. Flowers in an umbel at end of a leafless flower stalk. Flowers with 3 sepals, 3 petals (usually both sepals and petals colored), stamens usually 3, pistil of 3 united carpels. The ovary is inferior usually and the fruit is a capsule or a berry with many seeds. Approximately 10 taxa of the family are known outside cultivation in Arkansas; numerous additional species are cultivated. The large-flowered Amaryllis of winter pot plants belong to the family, as do Crinum "lilies" and Narcissus and Jonquils.

Iris Family   *Iridaceae*
Perennial herbs with bulbs, rhizomes, or corms. Leaves usually alternate, simple, basal, and with prominent sheathing bases and parallel venation. Flowers, usually, with a perianth of 6 colored petallike parts, 3 stamens, and an inferior ovary with 3 united carpels. About 17 taxa of the family are found as horticultural subjects. Crocus, Iris or Flag, and Gladiolus are members of this family.

Arrowroot Family   *Marantaceae*
Herbs of wet places, with pinnately veined leaves, long-petioled leaves having ovate lanceolate blades of relatively large size, and open panicles of showy purple flowers. Sepals 3, petals 3, stamens 3. Most parts of the plant are covered by a white-powdery bloom that can be easily rubbed from the surface. Represented in Arkansas by a single species, *Thalia dealbata*. No cultivated members of the family are well-known.

Orchid Family   *Orchidaceae*
Perennial herbs, often epiphytic, of a variety of habitats. Leaves alternate usually,rarely opposite or whorled, simple, sometimes much reduced. Flowers with 3 sepals, 3 petals, 1-2 stamens, and a pistil of 3 united carpels. Flowers have a markedly bilateral symmetry and one of the petals usually is modified as a lip. Ovary is inferior. This family is represented in Arkansas by about 40 taxa. Native species of this family are marked by beautiful and often somewhat bizarre flowers, and the cultivated members are equally beautiful and interesting. Most people are familiar with the Cattleya flowers of the florist's corsage; many do not know, however, that vanilla flavoring is extracted from the seed pods of the vanilla orchid (native to the American tropics).

Family Descriptions

Dicotyledons

(Dicots)

Plants with two seed leaves (cotyledons). The flower parts are usually in fours or fives or in multiples of these numbers. The leaves usually have net veins (palmate or pinnate).

A total of 67 families of plants is included from the Dicotyledon group. These contain most of the showy herbaceous wildflowers from this group in Arkansas.

Tree species are not included. Some the more showy vine and shrub species are treated.

All of Arkansas' showy dicot species that are being cultivated are perennials except where otherwise indicated.

FAMILY DESCRIPTIONS

DICOTYLEDONS

Lizard's-tail Family   *Saururaceae*

Succulent perennial herbs with jointed stems and alternate entire leaves. Flowers very small, without a perianth, crowded into a slender spike that is nodding at the tip. This is a small family comprised of only about 7 species in North America and Asia. It is represented in Arkansas by a single species, *Saururus cernuus*, Lizard's-tail, a very aromatic plant growing in water or muddy soils. Our native species is of no known economic significance as is the case with other species of the family.

Sandalwood Family   *Santalaceae*

A family of trees, shrubs, and herbs (herbs only in Arkansas). Represented in Arkansas by a single species, *Comandra umbellata*, Bastard toadflax, which is a perennial herb with alternate, entire leaves and a root-parasite on a number of species in different plant families. Flowers are white, or greenish-white, small, in corymbose clusters, and with an inferior ovary. The family is represented in Eurasia and North America by a total of several hundred species in about 30 genera, none of which are of particular importance.

Birthwort Family   *Aristolochiaceae*

Twining woody vines or small herbaceous plants, mostly with alternate heart-shaped leaves. Flowers of the family are interesting for their markedly bilaterally symmetrical character, causing them to resemble an old-fashioned Dutch pipe, hence the common name of Dutchman's pipe for many members of the family. Flowers usually are brownish or purplish in color and are characterized by having sepals and petals in 3's, a character more often associated with monocots than dicots. The family is primarily tropical in distribution but is represented in Arkansas by about 5 taxa. There are few cultivated members of the family.

Smartweed Family   *Polygonaceae*

Mostly herbs (although sometimes woody), with mostly alternate leaves and swollen nodes, a membranous sheath called an ocrea forming a collar around each node, and often with a watery, acrid juice in the stems and leaves. Flowers are usually bisexual, small in size, with petaloid sepals and lacking petals, and a lens-shaped or triangular achene for a fruit. This family of about 800 species in 40 genera is most widespread in North Temperate areas. Over 30 species of the family occur in Arkansas outside cultivation. Economic plants of the family include rhubarb, buckwheat, and sea grape, a commonly cultivated shrub in tropical areas. Members of the genus *Polygonum* are among the most common of our weeds.

Amaranth Family   *Amaranthaceae*

Annual or perennial herbs or shrubs (but usually herbs), leaves alternate or opposite, simple, and both stems and leaves are often marked by prominent reddish or purplish pigments. Flowers are minute, usually greenish in color, and often associated with dry, papery or prickly bracts. Sepals are 5 in number and petals are lacking. Fruit usually few seeded. The family includes over 500 species and is widely distributed in temperate and warm areas of the world. Cockscomb and Globe amaranth are commonly cultivated ornamentals of the garden, while numerous members of the family are noxious weeds, particularly in dry areas. Approximately 15 species of the family occur in Arkansas.

Four-O-clock Family   *Nyctaginaceae*

Our plants of the family are perennial herbs with opposite, simple, entire leaves. The flowers consisting of 5 sepals and no petals commonly are associated with brightly colored bracts that resemble sepals; the brightly colored sepals in turn resemble petals. Except for a few ornamentals, such as Four-O-clock and Bougainvillea, the family is of little economic importance. Three members of the family occur in the Arkansas flora.

Pokeweed Family   *Phytolaccaceae*

Our member of the family is an erect herb with alternate, simple, entire leaves. Flowers are relatively small, bisexual, with 5 sepals and lacking petals. The fleshy fruits have a multicarpellate structure with several seeds and are marked by reddish or purplish juice. The family is mostly found in the tropics and is represented in Arkansas by a single species, *Phytolacca americana*, Pokeweed. Some members of the family are cultivated as ornamentals but generally the group is of little economic significance.

Purslane Family   *Portulacaceae*

Annual or perennial herbs, usually with fleshy leaves. Flowers are bisexual, with radial symmetry, a calyx of 2 sepals, corolla of 4-6 petals, and stamens of variable number. The fruits have no subdivisions within and usually contain several seeds; the fruit often splits by means of a lid that breaks away from the top of the fruit. The family is chiefly American in distribution and is well distributed along the West Coast of the U. S. The family is of little economic importance, but some members such as the commonly cultivated Rose moss or Portulaca are ornamentals.

Pink Family   *Caryophyllaceae*

Annual or perennial herbs with opposite, simple leaves connected by a transverse line. Flowers often are showy, usually have flower parts in 5's, and have a superior ovary that usually matures into a many-seeded capsule. The family is widespread in cool or North Temperate parts of the world and contains numerous weedy species as well as many cultivated ornamentals. Cultivated species include Carnation, Pinks, Sweet William, and Baby's Breath.

Water Lily Family   *Nymphaeaceae*

Perennial aquatic herbs with long-petioled leaves that usually are simple, alternate, floating or emersed, and roundish in outline. Flowers are bisexual, usually solitary and showy, and with a perianth of numerous sepals and petals that are poorly differentiated. The family is widely distributed through the world in aquatic habitats. Many members of the family are important in the food chains of many kinds of birds and wildlife species. Some members of the family are grown as ornamentals in aquatic gardens or fishponds. Six species of the family occur in Arkansas.

Crowfoot or Buttercup Family   *Ranunculaceae*

Annual or perennial herbs, leaves usually alternate, compound, and with prominently sheathing leaf bases. Flowers may be solitary or in groups, are mostly bisexual, regular or irregular in symmetry. The perianth usually is petaloid, with the sepals and petals poorly if at all differentiated, and the stamens and carpels usually are numerous. Flowers often are blue, yellow, or white. The family is very large and most widespread in the cooler portions of the northern hemisphere. The family contains numerous poisonous species, many drug plants, and countless ornamentals. Cultivated members of the family include Columbine, Peony, Anemone, and Larkspur. Approximately 50 members of the family occur in Arkansas.

Barberry Family   *Berberidaceae*

Both species of the family listed for Arkansas are herbaceous with simple or compound leaves. The flowers are radially symmetrical with 4-6 sepals that are often petallike, 4-8 petals, stamens as many as or twice as many as the petals and arranged in two circles. The pollen sacs open by means of tiny lids. The fruit is a berry or capsule from the single pistil. A small family that is scattered through the north temperate zone. A few species are used as ornamentals.

Poppy Family   *Papaveraceae*

Annual or perennial herbs with alternate, entire or divided leaves, and usually with milky or colored latex in stems and leaves. Flowers are bisexual, showy, regular in symmetry, usually with 2 sepals that fall quickly after the flower opens and several separate petals that are crumpled in the bud. Stamens are numerous and the fruit is a capsule opening by valves or pores. The family occurs chiefly in the North Temperate and tropical regions. The family is the source of many ornamentals and drug plants, such as Opium poppy, Iceland poppy, and Oriental poppy. Five species of the Poppy family grow outside cultivation in Arkansas.

Fumitory Family *Fumariaceae*

Delicate herbs or climbers with alternate, compound leaves and watery juice. Flowers usually are irregular, bisexual, and with a superior ovary. Sepals are 2, falling soon after the flower opens. Petals are 4, in two pairs of different sizes, while stamens are 4-6. The ovary of 2 united carpels matures into a many-seeded capsule. The family is especially widespread in the Mediterranean region, but is represented in Arkansas by only four species. A few species are cultivated as ornamentals, but the family generally is of little economic significance.

Mustard Family *Cruciferae*

Annual or perennial herbs, with leaves usually alternate, simple to highly dissected, and with watery, acrid juices. Flowers are bisexual, regular in symmetry, and usually in racemes. The sepals and petals are 4 in number, while the stamens are 6 (4 long and 2 short). The ovary consists of 2 united carpels and matures into a fruit called either a silicle or a silique (depending on relation between length and width of fruit). The mature fruit is of extreme importance in accurate identification of some species in this family. The family is well developed in temperate and cold regions of the world. Many members of the family are noxious weeds, some are garden vegetables, and others are ornamental. Cultivated members include Cabbage, Broccoli, Turnip, Radish, and Mustard. About 60 species of the family occur outside cultivation in Arkansas.

Caper Family *Capparaceae*

Herbs with alternate, simple or compound leaves. Flowers usually have flower parts mostly in 4's, and the petals usually are long-clawed (looking as though they have a petiole). Stamens usually are much exserted from the flower. Flowers usually are irregular in symmetry and marked by an ovary that is on a stalk. The ovary matures into a many-seeded capsule. The family is widespread through tropical and subtropical parts of the world. Several species, such as Cleome or Spider plant, are important ornamentals, while the Caper bush is the source of capers for salads. Only three species of the family occur in Arkansas.

Stonecrop Family *Crassulaceae*

Succulent herbs with simple, opposite or alternate leaves. Flowers are bisexual, usually have 5 sepals and 5 petals, regular symmetry, and 5 more or less free carpels. The fruit usually is a group of follicles, sometimes a capsule. The family is widely distributed in South Africa, as well as in western North America. The family is of little economic importance except for some ornamentals, such as Sedum, Houseleek, Jade plant, and Kalanchoc. Six species of the family occur in Arkansas.

Sundew Family *Droseraceae*

Plants of mostly wet, acid habitats. Usually having a basal rosette of leaves, which are modified by the presence of large stalked glands for the capture of insects. Flowers are showy, bisexual, regular in symmetry, and with 5 sepals and 5 petals. The flowers usually are in cymes atop a leafless flower stalk. The family contains a relatively small number of species but is widely distributed. The group is of no economic significance but is a curiosity because of the insect-catching potential of the species. A single species of the family occurs in Arkansas.

Saxifrage Family *Sarifragaceae*

Perennial herbs with alternate,.usually palmately- veined and -lobed leaves. Flowers are bisexual, regular in symmetry, and usually in racemose or cymose inflorescences. The sepals usually are 5 as are the petals; stamen number usually is 5 or 10, and the pistil is composed of 2-5 carpels. The flowers have the ovary contained within a hypanthium or floral cup. The family is widespread in the cooler and temperate areas of the Northern Hemisphere, and is represented in Arkansas by about 20 species. Several members of the family, such as many species of the genus *Savifraga*, are cultivated as rock garden subjects.

Rose Family
Rosaceae

The Rose family is a large and variable family. In general the family may be described as consisting of herbs, shrubs, or trees with leaves alternate, simple or compound, and with prominent stipules. Flowers usually are regular, have 5 sepals, 5 petals, many stamens, and a variable number of carpels. Fruits are highly variable in the family, ranging from dry capsules and follicles to fleshy drupes and pomes. The family is widespread in the Northern Hemisphere and contains many species of economic significance. Common members of the family include Rose, Blackberry, Strawberry, Quince, Apple, Peach, Plum, and Cherry. The Arkansas flora has many members of the family.

Pea, Bean, or Legume Family
Leguminosae

The Legume family is a large and variable family. Generally the family may be described as consisting of herbs, shrubs, or trees with leaves alternate, simple or compound, and with prominent stipules. Flowers may be either regular or irregular in symmetry, with 5 sepals and 5 petals, with 10-many stamens, and an ovary with one carpel. The fruit usually is a beanlike pod, called a legume. The family is widespread in occurrence and contains many economically significant species, such as Mimosa, Redbud, Bean, and Pea. Many members of the family occur in Arkansas.

Flax Family
Linaceae

Slender herbs in Arkansas with the flowers on forked branches. There are 5 separate sepals and 5 separate petals, 10 stamens joined at the base. The petals drop soon after blooming. The simple slender leaves are alternate or opposite and the fruit is usually a 5-chambered capsule. Various species occur over most of the world. In this state 3 species occur outside cultivation. Linseed oil and linen are products of the family.

Wood Sorrel Family
Oxalidaceae

Mostly perennial herbs with alternate, trifoliolately compound leaves, usually with a sour taste to leaves and stems. Flowers are bisexual, regular in symmetry, and in umbels. The sepals are 5, petals are 5, and stamens are 10 and fused by their filaments. The ovary is superior, and it matures into a capsule that contains many seeds, often being released explosively. The family is of widespread occurrence, particularly in the tropics, but is of little economic importance. Some species, particularly of the genus *Oxalis*, are cultivated as ornamentals.

Geranium Family
Geraniaceae

Herbs with alternate or opposite, simple or compound leaves; the venation is often palmate as is lobing of the leaves. Flowers are bisexual, regular in symmetry, and occur in umbels. Sepals are 5, petals are 5, and stamens are 5-15. The fruit is a long-beaked elastic capsule, which splits and releases its seeds, often explosively. The family is widespread in temperate regions and includes a number of cultivated ornamentals, including the commonly cultivated Geranium of window boxes and flower pots.

Milkwort Family
Polygalaceae

Herbs with alternate, opposite, or whorled, simple leaves. Flowers bisexual, irregular in symmetry, and usually in racemes, spikes, or panicles. Flowers resembling the pealike flowers of the Legume family. The family is widespread in distribution but is of little economic importance. About 9 species of the family occur in Arkansas.

Spurge Family
Euphorbiaceae

Mostly herbs with milky juice in all parts of the plants. Leaves usually simple and alternate. Flowers are typically unisexual and minute but often are associated with showy bracts or other modified structures that appear to make the flowers more showy. The family is extremely large, particularly in tropical areas. Some species of the family closely resemble cactus plants. Economically important products of the family include natural rubber, tapioca, and castor oil. Ornamental species of the family include Christmas poinsettia. Numerous species of the family occur in Arkansas.

Touch-me-not or Balsam Family   *Balsaminaceae*

Succulent herbs with watery stems, alternate or opposite leaves, and somewhat swollen nodes. Flowers are bisexual, prominently irregular in symmetry and with an elongated tubular spur. Sepals 5, petals 5, stamens 5, and a pistil with 5 united carpels. The fruit is an explosive capsule, hence the common name of "touch-me-not" for many members of the family. The family is of little importance, although some members of the genus *Impatiens* are cultivated as ornamentals.

Buckthorn Family   *Rhamnaceae*

Mostly trees, shrubs, or woody vines. Leaves usually alternate and with prominent veins. Flowers are small, in cymes, marked by flower parts in 5's and the presence of a hypanthium or floral cup. The family is of little economic importance, althouigh edible fruits are produced by Jujube and a laxative is produced by Cascara or Buckthorn. The family is of little importance in the Arkansas flora.

Mallow Family   *Malvaceae*

Mostly herbs with alternate, simple, palmately veined leaves. Flowers usually are showy, with flower parts in 5's except for the many stamens, which are fused into a column by their filaments. The pistil consists of several to many carpels, these united into a ring and containing several seeds. The fruit usually is a capsule that splits open at maturity. The family is important in tropical areas of the world and contains many species of economic significance. Cotton, Okra, and Hollyhock are all members of the family.

St. John's-wort Family   *Hypericaceae*

Herbs or shrubs with simple, opposite or whorled, entire leaves, the leaves usually being glandular- dotted. Flowers usually are yellow or orange, showy, and in cymes. Sepals and petals usually are in 4's or 5's, while the stamens are numerous and grouped into bunches. The pistil has 1 cavity and contains many seeds of small size. The family is relatively small and found in both temperate and tropical areas. Some members of the family are noxious weeds, including some which are poisonous to livestock. Others are ornamentals.

Rockrose Family   *Cistaceae*

Herbs with leaves simple, alternate, opposite, or whorled, entire. Flowers are bisexual, regular in symmetry, and with a superior ovary. Sepals and petals are 3-5, while stamens are few to numerous. The pistil consists of few to several carpels that are united. The petals of some species are very showy but are insignificant in others. The family is relatively small and is found in both temperate and subtropical areas of the world. The group is of little economic significance.

Violet Family   *Violaceae*

Annual or perennial herbs; leaves either alternate or basal and with prominent stipules. Flowers are solitary or in groups, mostly irregular in symmetry, usually with a hypanthium or floral cup, and with a prominent spur on the undersides of the flower. Flower parts are mostly in 5's, and the superior ovary consists of 3 united carpels. The fruit is a several- to many-seeded capsule. The family is widely distributed, and in Arkansas is represented by over a dozen species. Some members of the family are cultivated as ornamentals. The common Violet and Pansy are members of the family.

Passion-flower Family   *Passifloraceae*

Mostly herbaceous tendril-bearing vines with alternate, lobed leaves. Flowers are bisexual, regular in symmetry, and axillary in position. Sepals and petals usually are 5, while the stamens are often more numerous. A corona of threadlike filaments surrounds the stamens. The ovary is superior and consists of 3 united carpels. The fruit is a berry with many seeds. The family is primarily tropical in distribution, with only a few species in temperate regions. Cultivated members of the family include Passion Fruit and Granadilla, both of which are sources of edible fruits in the tropics.

Loasa Family   *Loasaceae*

Herbs with leaves and stems covered with rough, sometimes stinging hairs. Flowers usually have flower parts in 5's, except for the many stamens and 1-celled ovary. The fruit is a many-seeded capsule. The family is well-developed in the drier parts of the American Southwest. The genus *Mentzelia*, or Blazing Star, is often cultivated as an ornamental, but otherwise the family is of little importance.

Cactus Family   *Cactaceae*

Perennial plants, generally without true leaves on mature stems, the stems thickened but flattened and covered with spines. Flowers solitary, bisexual, usually regular in symmetry, with a hypanthium or floral cup. Sepals and petals not clearly differentiated. Stamens numerous, while the pistil is of 3-several carpels but with only 1 opening. The fruit is a fleshy berry. The family is of widespread occurrence, primarily in the western hemisphere. It is of little economic importance other than the source of numerous ornamentals, which are grown by the cactus or succulent fancier.

Loosestrife Family   *Lythraceae*

Herbs and woody plants with leaves opposite or whorled, simple, entire. Flowers bisexual, regular or irregular, with a hypanthium or floral cup. Flowers 4-to 7-parted. The fruit is a dry capsule. The family is mostly restricted to the tropics. Many members of the family are associated with wetlands, and a few species are cultivated as ornamentals. The cultivated Crepe myrtle is one of the best known species in the family.

Melastoma or Meadow Beauty Family   *Melastomataceae*

Herbs with simple, opposite leaves and showy flowers arranged in cymes. Flowers bisexual, regular in symmetry, mostly with flower parts in 4's or 5's except for stamens which are twice as many as petals. This is a large tropical family with a relatively few Arkansas representatives. The family is of little economic significance.

Evening Primrose Family   *Onagraceae*

Herbs with simple, alternate, or opposite leaves. Flowers bisexual, regular or irregular in symmetry, with an inferior ovary, flower parts mostly in 4's and with stamens as many or twice as many as petals. The fruit usually is a capsule. The family is of little economic significance except for a few ornamentals, such as Fuchsia.

Ginseng Family   *Araliaceae*

Herbs or shrubs and small trees with leaves alternate, palmately or pinnately compound, and with sheathing leaf bases. Flowers small and insignificant, with flower parts usually in 4's or 5's and with an inferior ovary. The fruit is a berry, often brightly colored. The group is primarily a tropical family. Some species of the family, such as Fatsia and Schefflera, are prized ornamentals. Other species, such as Ginseng, are of medicinal value. The family is represented in Arkansas by very few species.

Carrot or Parsley Family   *Umbelliferae*

Biennial or perennial herbs, usually very aromatic and marked by alternate or basal leaves that usually are compound and with markedly dilated petiole bases. Stems usually are hollow. Flowers usually have flower parts in 5's except for the pistil with 2 united carpels. Flowers are in umbels, and the fruit type is a schizocarp. The family, of widespread occurrence in the northern hemisphere, is of much economic importance because of numerous culinary herbs, food plants, poisonous species, and ornamentals. Members of the family include Coriander, Celery, Parsley, Dill, and Poison Hemlock. Numerous members of the family occur in Arkansas.

Wintergreen Family   *Pyrolaceae*

Perennial herbs, represented in Arkansas by a single genus of fleshy herbs that are parasitic on other plants. Plants lacking chlorophyll and with flowers that are bisexual, regular in symmetry, and with a superior ovary. The fruit is a capsule. The family is found in moist woods of the northern hemisphere. The family is of no economic significance.

Heath Family   *Ericaceae*

Woody plants with mostly alternate, entire, often leathery leaves. Flowers bisexual, regular or irregular in symmetry, having 4-5 fused sepals and 4-5 fused petals. Fruit a many-seeded capsule. This family is mostly restricted to acid soils and contains numerous economically important plants. Heather, Azalea, Wintergreen, and Blueberry belong to the Heath family.

Primrose Family   *Primulaceae*

Annual or perennial herbs with opposite, basal, or whorled leaves. Flowers have flower parts in 5's, and the ovary is either superior or half-inferior. A few ornamental species, such as Cyclamen and Primrose, belong to the family, but generally it is of little economic significance. The family is mostly found in the north temperate regions of the world.

Logania Family   *Loganiaceae*

Herbs or woody vines with opposite leaves. Flowers bisexual, regular in symmetry, with flower parts in 5's and with marked fusion of petals into a tube, stamens fused to inside of petal tube. Fruit a capsule with many seeds. The family primarily occurs in warm regions of the world and only four species occur in Arkansas. The family is of little economic significance.

Gentian Family   *Gentianaceae*

Annual or perennial herbs with opposite, entire leaves. Flowers bisexual, regular in symmetry, with 4-5 unfused sepals, 4-5 united petals, 4-5 stamens fused to inside of petal tube. Ovary of 2 united carpels, maturing into a many-seeded capsule. Worldwide in distribution, with about 14 species in Arkansas. Of little or no economic significance other than cultivation of some species as ornamentals.

Dogbane Family   *Apocynaceae*

Herbs or small shrubs with leaves opposite or whorled, simple, entire, and with milky juice. Flowers bisexual, regular in symmetry, with flower parts usually in 5's, the petals united into a tube, stamens attached to inside of petal tube. Ovary of 2 carpels, either separate or united. Fruit usually 2 follicles, the seeds usually hairy. A family found mainly in warm regions of the world, with 10 species in Arkansas. The group contains a number of poisonous species, some of importance in poisoning livestock and others used in the drug industry. Some members, such as Oleander, Periwinkle, and Frangipani, are prized as ornamentals.

Milkweed Family   *Asclepiadaceae*

Herbs with leaves alternate, opposite, or whorled, simple, entire, and with milky juice. Flowers bisexual, regular in symmetry, with flower parts usually in 5's, the petals united into a tube. The petals often with a set of appendages forming a petallike corona. Stamens 5 but much modified, attached to stigma, pollen united into waxy bodies called pollinia. Carpels 2, the ovaries separate but styles and stigma united, each carpel forming a fruit usually. Flowers usually in umbels. Fruit a follicle, with numerous seeds having a tuft of silky hairs at one end. A mostly tropical family, but with about 21 species in Arkansas. The family is of only moderate economic importance as a source of natural rubber, ornamentals, fibers, poisonous plants, and a few food items. Several species are poisonous to livestock and others cause severe dermatitis in humans. The flower structure in this family is usually termed "bizarre" and is highly suited to insect pollination.

Morning Glory Family   *Convolvulaceae*

Mostly trailing vines with leaves alternate and simple, usually with milky juice. Flowers with flower parts in 5's, petals fused into a plaited tube, stamens attached to inside of petal tube, ovary with 2 united carpels. Fruit a capsule, usually. A family of mostly warm regions of the world, with over 25 species in Arkansas. A few species are noxious weeds, and a number of the parasitic members are destructive of certain crop plants. A few species are cultivated as ornamentals. The Morning Glory and Sweet Potato belong to the family.

Phlox Family   *Polemoniaceae*

Mostly annual or perennial herbs, leaves alternate or opposite. Flowers usually showy, in cymes, flower parts usually in 5's and united, stamens fused to inside of petal tube, ovary of 3 united carpels. Fruit a many-seeded capsule. This family is especially well-represented in the western parts of North America, and many species occur in alpine regions. Many members of the family are cultivated as ornamentals; included are Phlox, Standing cypress, Jacob's ladder, and Cup-and-saucer vine. Flowers in the family usually are pink, blue, purple, or some related color.

Waterleaf Family   *Hydrophyllaceae*

Herbs with leaves alternate or opposite, often with basal rosettes, often with bristly, glandular, or otherwise harsh surfaces. Flowers bisexual, regular in symmetry, with flower parts in 5's, sepals and petals fused into tubes, usually arranged in cymes, particularly cymes that are coiled. Stamens attached to inside of petal tube, ovary of 2 united carpels, maturing into a many-seeded capsule usually. The family occurs mostly in North America, with about 15 species in Arkansas. The plant is of little importance, although a few members are cultivated as ornamentals.

Borage or Forget-me-not Family   *Boraginaceae*

Herbs with leaves alternate, simple, entire, usually covered with rough hairs of some type. Flowers bisexual, regular in symmetry, with flower parts in 5's, petals and usually sepals fused into tubes, stamens attached to inside of petal tube. Ovary superior and with 2 united carpels, usually maturing into 4 nutlets, each containing one seed. Flowers often blue, arranged in coiled cymes. The family occurs mostly in warm regions of the world, but relatively few members are of any economic significance. A few species, such as Comfrey and Borage, are cultivated as ornamentals and medicinal plants. Twenty-six species of the family occur in Arkansas.

Vervain Family   *Verbenaceae*

Herbs and shrubs with leaves opposite or whorled, simple, stems often square in outline. Flowers bisexual, with flower parts in 5's, irregular in symmetry, sepals and petals each united into tubes, stamens attached to inside of petal tube. Ovary superior and with 2 united carpels, not deeply lobed, and usually forming 2-4 nutlets in fruit. Widely distributed in warmer parts of the world, represented in Arkansas by about 17 species. A few species, such as Lantana, Verbena, and Teak are of economic importance.

Mint Family   *Labiatae*

Mostly strongly aromatic herbs with leaves opposite and simple, stems square in outline. Flowers bisexual, with flower parts in 5's, irregular in symmetry, sepals and petals each united into tubes, stamens attached to inside of petal tube. Stamens 2-4, ovary superior and of 2 united carpels, appearing to be deeply 4-lobed. Fruit four 1 -seeded nutlets surrounded by the persistent sepals. Flowers usually are borne in spikes having whorls of flowers. The family has a major center of distribution in the Mediterranean region, but is represented in the Arkansas flora by over 60 species. Many species of the family are economically important as ornamentals, culinary herbs, sources of aromatic oils used in perfumes and other fragrances, and a few are weeds. Common members of the family are Peppermint, Sage, Thyme, Lavender, and Coleus.

Nightshade Family   *Solanaceae*

Mostly herbs with leaves alternate and simple, herbage often rank-smelling. Flowers bisexual, regular or irregular in symmetry, flower parts in 5's, grouped in cymes. Sepals 5 and united, petals 5 and united, stamens usually 5 and attached to inside of petal tube, ovary superior and with 2 united carpels. Fruit commonly a capsule or a berry. This family has a major center of distribution in South America but occurs worldwide. Over 15 species occur in Arkansas. Important plants of the family are Potato, Tomato, Tobacco, Petunia, and Bell pepper. Many of the plants in this family contain poisonous alkaloids, making many species important drug sources.

Figwort or Snapdragon Family   *Scrophulariaceae*

Mostly herbs with leaves alternate, opposite, or whorled. Many members of the family are at least partially parasitic on the root system of other species. Flowers with flower parts usually in 5's except for stamens usually 4, irregular in symmetry, ovary superior and with 2 united carpels. Flowers usually in cymes or racemes. Fruit usually a capsule with numerous seeds. Members of this family may be confused with those of the Mint family (which never has a capsule with numerous seeds). This family is of wide distribution, and there are about 57 species known in Arkansas. The family is the source of Digitalis and Snapdragon.

Trumpet Creeper Family   *Bignoniaceae*

Mostly woody plants with leaves opposite, simple or compound. Flowers are showy, with flower parts in 5's and very similar to those of the Snapdragon family. Fruit a capsule, often containing seeds that are winged. Widely distributed in the tropics, with a major center of distribution in Brazil. The family is a source of lumber and a few ornamentals, but relatively few are known outside the tropics except for Catalpa. Only 5 species in Arkansas.

Broomrape Family   *Orobanchaceae*

Herbs that are root parasites on other species, with much reduced leaves, and little or no green color. Flower structure is similar to that found in the Snapdragon family. The family is of no economic importance. Two species of the family occur in Arkansas.

Bladderwort Family   *Lentibulariaceae*

Mostly aquatic herbs with leaves alternate or in rosettes. The leaves are modified with small traps that catch and digest various forms of microscopic aquatic animal life. Flower structure is similar to that found in the Snapdragon Family. The family is of wide distribution, but only 4 species are known in Arkansas. The group is of little or no economic importance.

Acanthus Family   *Acanthaceae*

Herbs with leaves opposite and simple. Cystoliths (deposits of calcium carbonate) often are present as bumps or streaks in the vegetative parts of the plant. Flowers bisexual, irregular in symmetry, with flower parts in 4's or 5's, petals usually united into a two-lipped tube, stamens attached to inside of petal tube. Ovary superior, usually maturing into a many-seeded capsule. Widespread, particularly in the tropics. A few members of the family, such as Shrimp plant, are cultivated as ornamentals.

Lopseed Family   *Phrymaceae*

Perennial herbs with slender stems and opposite toothed leaves. Flowers bisexual, irregular in symmetry, with flower parts mostly in 5's except for 4 stamens and a superior ovary of 1 cell and 1 seed. Only a single species known in Arkansas from the family. Of no economic importance.

Plantain Family   *Plantaginaceae*

Annual or perennial herbs with basal rosettes of parallel-veined leaves and spikes of flowers atop leafless flower stalks. Flowers with flower parts in 4's, sepals and petals each united into tubes, stamens attached to inside of petal tube. Petals usually are papery in texture. Fruit usually a capsule that is circumscissile (the top part of the fruit splits away much in the form of a lid). Seeds often are mucilaginous, and one species is the source of a laxative made from the seeds. Of little importance other than the fact that many species are lawn weeds.

Bedstraw or Madder Family   *Rubiaceae*

Herbs or shrubs with leaves opposite or whorled, simple, usually entire. Stipules usually are present and often are leaflike. Flowers bisexual, usually regular in symmetry, with flower parts in 4's or 5's, petals united into a tube. Ovary inferior, composed of 2 united carpels. Fruit usually a capsule or a berry. Of wide occurrence in the tropics, and with over 30 species in Arkansas. The family is of importance as the source of coffee, quinine, and numerous ornamentals, such as Gardenia.

Honeysuckle Family   *Caprifoliaceae*

Mostly herbs or vines with opposite leaves and without stipules. Flowers bisexual, regular or irregular in symmetry, usually with flower parts in 5's, petals fused into a tube. Stamens attached to inside of petal tube. Ovary inferior, of 2-5 united carpels, commonly maturing into a berry. The family is of widespread occurrence in north temperate areas of the world, and about 15 species occur in Arkansas. Most of the genera in the family are in cultivation. Important members are Elderberry, Viburnum, and Honeysuckle.

Valerian Family   *Valerianaceae*

Annual or perennial herbs with leaves opposite or in basal rosettes. Flowers bisexual usually, irregular in symmetry, usually in cymes. Sepals are absent, and the 5 petals are united. Stamens are 1-4 and attached to the inside of the petal tube. The ovary is inferior and typically matures into a 1-seeded achene. The family is widespread in North Temperate regions and the Andes; represented in Arkansas by 5 species. Of little importance except for a very few cultivated members, such as Spikenard, the source of an unguent much used by the ancient Romans.

Teasel Family   *Dipsacaceae*

Herbs with leaves opposite and herbage often covered with prickly surfaces. Flowers bisexual, irregular in symmetry, in dense heads. Flowers with flower parts in 4's or 5's, stamens attached to inside of petal tube. Ovary inferior, of 2 united carpels, maturing into a 1-seeded achene. This Old World family is the source of several weedy species in the U.S. Members of the family often superficially resemble thistles (of the Composite or Sunflower Family). A single species, *Dipsacus fullonum*, Teasel, is represented in Arkansas.

Bellflower Family   *Campanulaceae*

Herbs with leaves usually alternate and simple, often. with milky juice. Flowers often showy, with flower parts in 5's, regular or irregular in symmetry, with petals united into a tube, stamens attached to inside of petal tube. Ovary of 2-5 united carpels, inferior or nearly so, usually maturing into a many-seeded capsule. A family of widespread occurrence and of little economic importance except for a few cultivated ornamentals. Bluebells and Balloon-flower belong to the family.

Composite or Sunflower Family   *Compositae*

This family ranks as one of the largest in the plant kingdom; approximately 10% of the species of flowering plants belong to the family. Because of its tremendous size it is difficult to generalize. Plants generally are herbs with alternate, opposite, or whorled leaves lacking stipules; leaves may be dissected but are never compound. Flowers usually occur in dense heads, the common receptacle of each head subtended by an involucre of several to many bracts. Each head usually resembles an individual flower, but actually the head is made up of few to numerous flowers, each of which has its own floral structure. Sepals are absent and often represented by hairlike or scalelike appendages, petals are 5 and united into a tube, the symmetry of the petal tube being either regular or irregular, stamens are 5 and united by the anthers. Members of the family, such as Sunflower, have a flower head consisting of a central disk composed of many tubular, regular flowers, while around the outside are "ray" flowers that are tubular but with irregular symmetry. Other members, such as Dandelion, have the head composed solely of tubular flowers with irregular symmetry. And yet others such as Ironweed, have all flowers of the head tubular and with regular symmetry. The ovary is inferior and contains a single seed after maturity into an achene. Many members of the family have the fruit capped by a set of hairs, scales, or bristles of some type, serving to aid in seed dispersal by wind. The family includes about 1,000 genera and nearly 25,000 species and is of worldwide distribution. It is the largest family in the Arkansas flora consisting of nearly 300 species. Members of the family of economic significance include Lettuce, Chicory, Artichoke, Chrysanthemum, and Sunflower.

MONOCOTYLEDONS

WATER-PLANTAIN FAMILY (Alismaceae)

A   CREEPING BURHEAD   *Echinodorus cordifolius*

The white flowers are borne on slender, arching flower stalks, are perfect (bisexual) and about ¹/₂ inch (13 mm) or less in width. The leaves are oval to somewhat heart-shaped and grow to about 1 foot (30 cm) high. Edges of ponds, canals, etc. Often in rice-growing areas. Central and northeastern counties. June-August.

* *Alisma plantago-aquatica*, Water Plantain, has very small flowers about ¹/₄ inch (6 mm) wide that are similar in shape to those of Creeping Burhead. They are carried on slender, leafless, profusely branching stems. The plants grow to about 2 feet (60 cm) high with basal, oval leaves on long petioles. Found mainly in northern and central counties in wet areas. May-August.

There are 6 species of the genus *Sagittaria* recorded in the state. Three of these are treated here. In this genus there is a great deal of variation in the leaf shapes, even within a single species. The flowers are all basically similar in appearance with the upper ones usually staminate (male).

B   GRASS-LEAVED ARROWHEAD   *Sagittaria graminea*

The flowers are ¹/₂ inch (13 mm) wide with yellow centers. They are borne in whorls of 3 on stalks that are taller than the leaves. The leaves are 1¹/₂ -2 feet (45-60 cm) tall and ¹/₂ inch (13 mm) wide with a milky juice. They are straight and slender, as indicated by the common name. Ditches, ponds, streams and near the edges of lakes and swamps. Nearly statewide. April-August.

C   BROAD-LEAVED ARROWHEAD, DUCK POTATO   *Sagittaria latifolia*

The flowers are large, 1 inch (2.5 cm) wide. The leaves are 2 feet (60 cm) or taller and of various shapes, the most common being the arrowhead form from which the plant derives one of its common names. Ducks and aquatic animals eat the starchy tubers. Shallow water or muddy areas, ditches, lakes, ponds. In scattered counties over most of the state. Summer months.

S. montevidensis, Giant Arrowleaf, has white petals with a purple spot at the base and the sepals are large. The pedicels are thick and the leaves are usually arrowheadshaped. Occurrence is scattered. June-September.

PALM FAMILY (Palmaceae)

This family is represented by only one species in Arkansas.

D   DWARF PALMETTO   *Sabal minor*

The flower cluster is up to 5 feet (1. 5 meters) long and branching with small yellowish blooms. The plant is a shrub up to 10 feet (3 meters) high with fan-shaped leaves divided into long, sharp-pointed segments. A variety of wet or dry, often sandy sites. Found mainly in extreme south Arkansas but also in low areas a third the way up the state in the Gulf Coastal Plain and Delta regions. April-June.

A

B

C

D

ARUM FAMILY (Araceae)

The 4 species from this family that are known to occur in Arkansas are shown.

A   SWEET FLAG   *Acorus americanus*

Tiny yellowish flowers are tightly packed on a conelike spadix which angles outward
from the bladelike stem. The flat, grasslike leaves are upright and up to 4 feet (1.2
meters) tall. Both the leaves and roots have a very pleasant aromatic odor, especially
when crushed. Ditches, marshes, swampy areas. Has been found in 9-10 counties in the
northern two-thirds of the state. Summer months.

B   JACK- IN-THE-PULPIT, INDIAN TURNIP   *Arisaema atrorubens*

The hood (spathe) or "pulpit" is pale green, often with purplish streaks on the inside
surface. The upright flower stalk (spadix) or "jack" averages 2-3 inches (5.0-7.5 cm) in
length and bears the tiny flowers. Flowering parts may be produced when the plant is
only a few inches (cm) tall. A cluster of red berries is produced at fruiting. Plants in the
southern part of the state and on better soils grow to 2 feet (60 cm) or more in height.
There are usually 2 compound leaves, each divided into 3 leaflets. Indians ate the
corms of these plants after drying and grinding them into a form of flour, and leaching
with water. Damp, rich woods. Statewide but apparently uncommon on alluvial soils.
March-May.

C   GREEN DRAGON, DRAGON ROOT   *Arisaema dracontium*

The flowers and flower parts are greenish to yellowish on the 3-5 inch (7.5-12.5 cm)
long spadix. The fruits are orange-red berries. These plants grow to well over 2 feet (60
cm) tall on good soils. There is one leaf divided into several leaflets with the main stem
curved or in a semicircle parallel to the ground. The corm of this plant was eaten by the
Indians. Moist woodlands. Over most of the state except for lowland soils. April-June.

D   ARROW ARUM   *Peltandra virginica*

A long green spathe tapers to a point and is wrapped closely around the spadix. The
large berries are dark green. The upright leaves are arrowhead- shaped with long, thick
petioles and are about 3 feet (1 meter) tall on fully grown plants. Marshes, shady
swamps. Collected in Lee, Lonoke, Monroe, Phillips, Nevada, Pulaski and Union
counties. April-June.

A

B

C

D

YELLOW-EYED GRASS FAMILY (Xyridaceae)

Five species, all in the genus *Xyris,* represent this family in Arkansas.

A   YELLOW-EYED GRASS   *Xyris spp.*

Yellow flowers about ½ inch (13 mm) wide are at the tops of the compact spikes which have brownish scales and somewhat resemble small pine cones. The leaves are up to 2 feet tall and ½ inch (13 mm) or less in width with flat blades. The seeds are eaten by ducks and quail. Wet pinelands, boggy areas, edges of streams and ponds. Recorded mainly in Ouachita Mountain and Gulf Coastal Plain Region counties. June-September.

PINEAPPLE FAMILY (Bromeliaceae)

Spanish-moss is the only species of the Pineapple Family known to occur in the state.

B   SPANISH-MOSS   *Tillandsia usneoides*

The small flowers are inconspicuous in the grayish masses of stringy stems and leaves and are first greenish to yellowish in color, later turning brown. There are small scales on the plants which catch the particles of dust and water that are necessary for growth. This species is not a true moss but actually a flowering plant and bears seeds. Hangs from trees, telephone lines and poles, other objects. Southernmost counties. May-July.

PIPEWORT FAMILY (Eriocaulaceae)

Two species from this family are listed for Arkansas.

C   HATPINS, PIPEWORT   *Eriocaulon decangulare*

The rounded, whitish flower heads are ¾ inch (18 mm) wide on tall, slender leafless stalks that are 2-2½ feet (60-75 cm) tall. There is a small black gland on each of the petal lobes. The leaves are in a basal rosette of grasslike blades about 6 inches (15 cm) long. Air pockets are visible in the leaves. Boggy areas, low pineland openings, edges of ponds. Known from Calhoun County only. July-September.

E. kornickianum resembles the above species but is only a few inches high. Found in a few northwestern counties, also Pulaski, Saline and Calhoun counties.

A

B

C

DAY-FLOWER FAMILY (Commelinaceae)

The 4 species of Day-flower occurring in Arkansas are well distributed throughout the state. Quail feed upon the seeds, especially of Slender Day-flower.

A ASIATIC DAY-FLOWER *Commelina communis*

The flowers are $^1/_2$ inch (13 mm) wide and light blue to more often deep blue, rarely white. Two rounded petals stand erect and the lower one is small and white. Flowers emerge from flat, folded sheaths and each lasts only a day. The foliage is deep green and up to 2 feet (60 cm) tall. The leaves are narrow and pointed, clasping the stem. A creeping plant with fibrous roots. There are often roots at the stem nodes. An annual that is native to Asia. Prefers damp areas both shaded and open. Nearly statewide except for overflow land and some alluvial soils. Spring into early fall.

C. erecta, Slender Day-flower, has more erect branching stems. A perennial with thick black roots but lacking a rhizome. Statewide.

B WOODS DAY-FLOWER, VIRGINIA DAY-FLOWER *Commelina virginica*

In this species the third petal is blue and nearly as large as the upper two. The plants are tall, erect perennials with large leaves and grow to be 3 feet (1 meter) tall. This species has a rhizome. Shady woodlands and edges, along streams. Statewide. Spring and early summer.

C. diffusa, Spreading Day-flower, has small flowers and plants and is an annual with branching, low-growing stems that often root at the nodes. Scattered over the state. Blooms during June-October.

There are 11 species and several hybrids of spiderwort reported from Arkansas. They are often browsed by deer and turkey.

C SPIDERWORT *Tradescantia spp.*

The illustration shows the form of growth of the more common species of the genus. Separation into the various species is often difficult in this genus.

T. ernestiana, is described as having varying shades of purple, rose or sometimes white blooms that are 1-1$^1/_2$ inches (2.5-3.8 cm) wide with bright yellow anthers. The colors are deeper than those of Ozark Spiderwort and the sepals are longer, without gland-tipped hairs. The plants are up to 2 feet (60 cm) tall with long, straight leaves that are pointed at the ends. The blades of the upper leaves are much wider than their sheaths, deep green in color and not glaucous (a white, powdery coating). Along roads, railroads, fields and woodland edges. Has been collected mainly from the western third of the state, also Ashley and Union counties. April into June. *T. occidentalis*, is similar but has more narrow leaves and is found mainly in the eastern half of the state, also in Sebastian, Pike and Nevada counties.

D HAIRY SPIDERWORT *Tradescantia hirsuticaulis*

The flowers are rose-colored or occasionally lavender. The plants are hairy, especially along the main stem, and the leaves are long and tapering. Open or thin woodlands, glades. Found mainly in the Ouachita Mountain and Gulf Coastal Plain regions, also Pope County. April-June.

A

B

C

D

A OHIO SPIDERWORT *Tradescantia ohiensis*

The flowers are usually a bright blue. The plants are tall with smooth stalks and bracts. The stems grow to 3 feet (1 meter) tall and are more upright and branching than those of other spiderwort species in Arkansas. Along roads, railroads, openings, fields. Statewide. May-July.

B OZARK SPIDERWORT *Tradescantia ozarkana*

Mainly white flowers edged with pink or white and having short sepals. The leaves are 1/2-2 inches (1.3-5 cm) wide, nearly hairless, grayish-green and more or less glaucous. The stems are somewhat hairy to nearly smooth. Fertile, rocky woodlands, slopes and ledges, especially on limestone soils. Mainly in Western Ozark Region counties, Polk and Montgomery counties in the Ouachita Mountain Region. April-May.

PICKEREL-WEED FAMILY (Pontederiaceae)

C MUD PLANTAIN, DUCK SALAD *Heteranthera limosa*

The blue flowers average 1½ inches (3.8 cm) in diameter. The smooth, deep-green leaves are oval with long petioles. The plants are sometimes submerged with only the flowers above the water line. Wet areas, streams, edges of lakes, marshes. Recorded in eastern counties and extreme northern counties, also Miller County. June-September.

D PICKEREL-WEED *Pontederia cordata*

The flowers are in terminal spikes about 6 inches (15 cm) long and are light blue to deep blue. The plants stand 3-4 feet(1-1.2 meters) above the water or mud. The leaves stand erectly, are lanceolate or heart-shaped and may be indented at the base. Ducks and aquatic animals feed on the seed pods. Widely scattered counties. April-October.

Eichhornia crassipes, Water Hyacinth, is a serious pest of waterways and is low-growing and free-floating or rooted in mud. The flower spike is similar to that of Pickerel-weed, but with larger, lighter-colored flowers. The leaves are rounded, often with inflated petioles. The plants usually die during severe winters. May have escaped in a few eastern counties where transplanted. Alien. May-September.

A

B

C

D

LILY FAMILY (Liliaceae)

A   UNICORN-ROOT, COLICROOT   *Aletris farinosa*

The white, tubular flowers are ¹/₂ inch (13 mm) long with a rough outer surface and orange stamens. The corolla is narrowed below the lobes. The flowers are carried on a long spike. The plants are up to 3 feet (1 meter) tall with a basal rosette of grasslike leaves and a few stem leaves. Woodland openings and roadsides in pinelands. Mainly in southern and central counties. April-June.

   A. aurea, Yellow Star-grass, a yellow version of the above, has been found in extreme southern Arkansas.

The genus *Allium* contains various species of wild and cultivated onions and garlic. Nine species have been recorded in Arkansas. All have the characteristic onion or garlic odor, especially when bruised.

B   WILD GARLIC, WILD ONION   *Allium canadense* var. *canadense*

Whitish, star-shaped flowers ¹/₄ inch (6 mm) long are in a somewhat rounded head. Small bulblets are often produced in the flower head; sometimes there are only flowers. The narrow, flattened leaves are mainly basal and not hollow. This species grows to about 2 feet (60 cm) tall and has a milder flavor than Field Garlic. The underground bulb is not divided into flat-sided segments. Open woods, fields, lawns. Statewide. May-July.

C   WILD GARLIC, PURPLE ONION   *Allium canadense* var. *mobilense*

There are white to pinkish flowers, often in a showy, globular inflorescence. This species is sometimes described as having flowers only - no bulblets. The pedicels are elongated. The plants grow to about 2 feet (60 cm) high. Prairies, glades, open areas in woodlands. In most of the counties in the northwestern part of the state, on the Grand Prairie and in a few eastern and southern counties. April-June.

   A. cernuum, Nodding Wild Onion, can be recognized by a curved upper flower stalk which causes the flowers to be carried in a nodding position. Recorded in 5 western counties. July-September. *A. vineale*, Field Garlic, has white to lavender flowers and long-tailed bulblets; sometimes the flowers are absent. The leaves are round and hollow and the underground bulb is divided into flat-sided segments. Found mainly in northern counties. A native of Europe. May-July.

D   WILD ONION, PRAIRIE ONION   *Allium stellatum*

The pink flowers are in spherical heads 2-2¹/₂ inches (5-6.3 cm) in diameter on stalks about 1 foot (30 cm) tall. Bulblets are not produced. Narrow, tubular leaves all grow from a bulb at the base of the plant. A variety of sites. Northern counties of the Ozark Region. Late summer and fall.

A

B

C

D

A WILD HYACINTH   *Camassia scilloides*

Pale blue or lavender flowers, rarely white, are 1 inch (2.5 cm) wide on an infloresence up to 10 inches (25 cm) or more in length. The flower stalks are leafless and occasionally reach 3 feet (1 meter) in height. The linear leaves are keeled. A variety of sites and soils. Ozark and Ouachita Mountain Region counties. Also on the Grand Prairie and in a few Gulf Coastal Plain Region counties. April-May.

B DEVIL'S BIT, FAIRY WAND   *Chamaelirium luteum*

The tiny male and female flowers are on separate plants in spikes 4-5 inches (10-12.5 cm) long. The female flowers are white. The male flowers appear creamy-white because of the yellowish stamens and are on shorter plants. The spikes usually droop near the tip. Reddish brown seeds are produced. This species sometimes reaches 3 feet (1 meter) in height with spatulate, evergreen, basal leaves which lie close to the ground. The leaves on the flower stalk are small and narrow. Near streams or lakes, banks of sloughs, swamps, rich, damp woodlands near seeps and springs but usually on fairly well drained sites. Eastern Ouachita Mountain and Gulf Coastal Plain Region counties. Rare. April-June.

C WHITE DOG-TOOTH VIOLET, WHITE TROUT LILY   *Erythronium albidum*

The white blooms have petals that curl back as they open; are solitary and 1 inch (2.5 cm) wide or slightly wider with large yellow stamens. The blooms often are in a nodding position. Most of the plants have single leaves. The flowers are on the two-leaved plants which have leaves up to about 6 inches (15 cm) long that are mottled with purplish brown suggesting the coloring of the trout. The name "dog-tooth" is derived from the shape of the bulb. Browsed by deer in early spring. Rich woods, along streams and on wooded slopes. Upland areas in the northern part of the state, also Polk and Monroe counties. February-April.

D YELLOW DOG-TOOTH VIOLET, YELLOW TROUT LILY *Erythronium rostratum*

Very similar to White Trout Lily but with erect yellow flowers on slightly larger plants. Occurs in many of the counties in the Ozark and Ouachita Mountain regions. Blooms later than White Trout Lily. March-May.

A

B

C

D

A   ORANGE DAY LILY   *Hemerocallis fulva*

Orange flowers with yellow centers are borne on leafless stalks. They average about 4 inches (10 cm) across and are not spotted. Each bloom lasts only one day. Double blossoms sometimes occur. The flower stalks are 3-5 feet (1-1.5 meters) high and are taller than the long, narrow leaves. This plant reproduces by the spreading of the roots and does not fruit. It is often found in thick colonies. A native of Europe and Asia that has been planted throughout the United States, Vacant lots and home places, roadsides, railroads. Northern and central counties. May-August.

B   MICHIGAN LILY   *Lilium michiganense*

Orange flowers with dull purplish dots are distributed over the top part of the older plants; often solitary on young plants. They are 2-3 inches (5-7.5 cm) wide with petals that curl as they open and hang face-downward with protruding style and stamens. The long, slender leaves are in whorls around the main stem which grows to about 6 feet (1.8 meters) tall. Moist wooded areas, prairies. Known from about 10 counties scattered over the northern and western parts of the state, also Clay, Green, Pulaski and Saline counties. June-July.

L. superbum, Turk's-cap Lily, a similar species, has been discovered in Arkansas, Logan, Pope and Stone counties. It has hairless leaf edges and veins, the midribs of the sepals are ribbed and the large anthers are fixed at the centers. The throat of the corolla is green.

C   BUNCH-FLOWER   *Melanthium virginicum*

The white flowers are ³/₄ inch (18 mm) wide with petals and sepals that are noticeably narrowed near the base and bear dark glands. The inflorescence is branched and spreading with the terminal flowers usually staminate (male). A tall plant that often grows to 7 feet (2.1 meters) high or higher with basal leaves up to 1¹/₂ feet (45 cm) in length that are slightly folded along the midrib. The stems are slightly hairy on the upper surface. Open or wooded, moist sites. Collected in 8 counties in the Ozark and Ouachita Mountain regions, also Calhoun and Saline counties. May-July.

Veratrum woodi, False Hellebore, has been recorded in only a few western counties. It is a tall plant when in bloom, with maroon, star-shaped flowers in a large panicle. As the flowers fade they take on green and purple tints. The rosette of large, smooth, oval, ribbed leaves is very noticeable in the woodlands, The plant does not bloom every year. The blooming period is July-September.

D   FALSE GARLIC, CROW POISON   *Nothoscordum bivalve*

White to pale yellowish flowers are at the tops of the flower stalks and each measures ¹/₂ inch (13 mm) across. The leaves are slender and upright with flat blades less than 1foot (30 cm) high. These plants are often in large colonies and do not have the onion or garlic odor. Nearly all types of open ground. Statewide. March-May, occasionally in the fall.

A

B

C

D

A   STAR OF BETHLEHEM   *Ornithogalum umbellatum*

White, upright flowers with pointed petals and sepals emerge from a thick clump of grasslike leaves with white midribs. The flowers are about 1 inch (2.5 cm) wide with a green stripe on the backside of each petal and sepal. The plants are usually less than 1 foot (30 cm) high. This native of Europe produces bulbs at a rapid rate. Grown in lawns and gardens, often escapes. Mainly in the northern half of the state. April-May.

0. nutans, Gray Lady, resembles the above but is more limited in distribution. The flowers are larger and nod as they age. The pedicels are much shorter than those of Star of Bethlehem.

B   SOLOMON'S SEAL   *Polygonatum biflorum*

The greenish-yellow tubular flowers hang in pairs or in groups of up to six below the arching stems, which often reach 5 feet (1.5 meters) in length. The flowers are ½ inch (13 mm) long or longer, with 6 lobes. The oval leaves are alternate on the stem and hairless, with conspicuous parallel leaf veins. Turkeys eat the fruits of this species. Usually in moist ground along streams, wooded slopes, valleys. Over most of the state; less common in the southeastern part. April-June.

C   SUNNYBELL   *Schoenolirion wrightii*

The small white to slightly yellowish flowers are closely grouped in a cylindrical inflorescence borne at the top of the flower stalk. The stamens are prominent. The leaves are slender, on plants slightly over 1 foot (30 cm) tall. There is a bulb below ground level with a taproot-like extension below it. Sandy soils, low pinelands. Known only from Ashley, Bradley, Calhoun, Cleveland and Drew counties in isolated locations. Rare. April-June.

D   FALSE SOLOMON'S SEAL   **Smilacina racemosa*

The tiny yellowish-white flowers are in a spreading terminal cluster. The fruits are red berries. The vegetative parts of this plant are similar to those of Solomon's Seal but the plants are only about 2 feet (60 cm) high. The leaves are slightly hairy underneath and the main stem of the plant is in a zig-zag shape. Occasionally browsed by deer. Damp woodlands. Nearly statewide but less frequent in the Delta Region. April-June.

A

B

C

D

A   FEATHERBELLS   *Stenanthium gramineum*

The small white flowers with slender, pointed petals and sepals hang downward in a many-flowered inflorescence which resembles a long feathery plume. The pedicels are shorter than the flowers. Most of the slender leaves are at the base of the 6-foot (1.8 meter) flower stalk and are slightly folded along the midrib. They are often over 1 foot (30 cm) long. Open woodlands. Known from Benton, Fulton, Independence, Stone and White counties in the Ozark Region, Montgomery and Polk counties in the Ouachita Mountain Region. June-August.

The genus *Trillium*, in Arkansas, contains 5 species. These plants grow on fertile soils of hill areas where there is a good moisture supply. All have whorls of three leaves below the flower. *Trillium* is one of the very few genera in the Monocotyledon class that does not have parallel leaf veins. All trilliums are perennial plants and often occur in large colonies. The leaves as well as the flowering parts, including the 3-parted pistil and 3 stigmas are in threes. The blooming period begins in early spring, before the trees are in full leaf.

B   WHITE-FLOWERED TRILLIUM   *Trillium flexipes*

A nodding white flower over 1 inch (2.5 cm) wide with creamy-white anthers is carried on a slender stalk above the leaves. A tall species with large, sessile leaves. Known from Stone County only.

C   OZARK WAKE ROBIN   *Trillium pusillum* var. *ozarkanum*

An upright, white, pink or wine-red flowered trillium with straight stamens and blunt leaves. The petals are in a flat position. The pink and red color phases occur as part of the fading process. Found in northwestern counties, Montgomery and Polk counties. Recent discovery of the species in western Pulaski County indicates that it may occur in other hill counties.

D   PURPLE TRILLIUM   *Trillium recurvatum*

The upright, sessile flower averages 1½ inches (3.8 cm) in length. It is usually maroon but various shades occur. The sepals are curved downward or recurved, hence the name "recurvatum." The petioled leaves are often mottled with dark shades of green. Nearly statewide except for some eastern and southern counties.

A

B

C

D

A   WAKE ROBIN, SESSILE TRILLIUM   *Trillium sessile*

The leaves are without petioles (sessile). Erect petals and sepals have variations in color intensity. Ozark and Ouachita Mountain regions, also Clark and Lee counties.

B   GREEN TRILLIUM   *Trillium viridescens*

Greenish flower parts. A somewhat larger plant than most trilliums, often well over 2 feet (60 cm) tall. Ozark and Ouachita Mountain regions, also Lonoke County.

C   LARGE-FLOWERED BELLWORT   *Uvularia grandiflora*

The yellow or pale yellow nodding flowers are $1\frac{1}{2}$ inches (3.8 cm) long and are smooth on the inside surface. Elongated, oval leaves are perfoliate and downy on the underside. A perennial plant up to 2 feet (60 cm) tall with a forked stalk. Usually has the appearance of suffering from lack of moisture. Fertile soil on wooded slopes and shelves. Well distributed over the Ozark Region and on Crowley's Ridge, also in a few Ouachita Mountain Region counties. Late March, April, May.

U. perfoliata, Perfoliate Bellwort, has flowers that are rough on the inside surface. The leaves are perfoliate. Recorded in Garland, Montgomery and Clay counties.

D   SMALL BELLWORT, SESSILE BELLWORT   *Uvularia sessilifolia*

The small, bell-shaped flower is pale yellow. The plants are less than 1 foot (30 cm) tall. Leaves are without petioles (sessile) and the stem is angled along the sides. Upland and well drained soils. Ozark and upland Ouachita Mountain Region counties, also Clay and Union counties. April-May.

Disporum lanuginosum, Yellow Mandarin, has nodding, greenish-yellow flowers with outcurved sepals and petals. The foliage is like that of Solomon's Seal. Occurs in Newton and nearby counties.

A

B

C

D

A ARKANSAS YUCCA, SOAPWEED *Yucca arkansana*

White to creamy-white flowers over 1 inch (2.5 cm) long are carried in a long, cylindrical inflorescence. The petals and sepals usually have blunt tips. The sepals are often pinkish. The leaves are mostly basal in a rosette of long, erect blades. The flower stalks grow to 6-7 feet (1.8-2.1 meters) tall. Two other species occur. Yuccas are often transplanted in Arkansas, sometimes from other states, and seem to be highly adaptable. Dry soils in upland areas, old fields, roadsides, yards and abandoned house sites. Ozark and Ouachita Mountain Region counties, also Little River County. Scattered elsewhere. May-October.

B DEATH CAMAS *Zigadenus nuttallii*

The perfect, white flowers are less than 1 inch (13 mm) wide and are closely grouped in a cylindrical head. There are 2 black glands at the base of each petal and sepal. This species is usually less than 3 feet (1 meter) high. The stems and leaves are smooth. Usually in dry, open areas. Northern counties, Little River and Sevier counties is the presently recorded range. April- May.

Amianthium muscaetoxicum, Fly Poison, is similar to Death Camas, but the pedicels are longer than the flowers. The rounded petals and sepals adhere to the fruits and turn green to purplish as they age. The flowers are about ¼ inch (6 mm) wide. Collected primarily from Ozark and Ouachita Mountain Region counties. April-May. See page 270.

AMARYLLIS FAMILY (Amaryllidaceae)

C FALSE ALOE, AGAVE *Agave virginica*

The fragrant green, brown and yellowish flowers are in spikes and each blossom is about 1 inch (2.5 cm) long. A large 3-parted capsule is produced at fruiting, which contains flat, black seeds which rattle when shaken, suggesting another of the common names for this species - " Rattlebox. " The tall, 6-foot (1.8 meter) flower stalks are surrounded at ground level with a thick whorl of leaves having pointed ends. The leaves are sometimes spotted. This is the only Arkansas species of a largely desert-inhabiting group of plants. Usually in dry situations such as rocky ledges, road banks, glades on both limestone and acid soils. Recorded in the northern two-thirds of the state; however, a recent collection from Columbia County indicates that the species is probably more widespread. Summer months.

D SPIDER LILY *Hymenocallis caroliniana*

White flowers of a distinctive spiderlike shape have stamens that protrude around the edge of the wide, central membrane. These flowers measure up to 8 inches (20 cm) across including the long lobes. One to several flowers occur on the twisted flower stalks. The plants are about 3 feet (1 meter) tall with long, linear leaves. The bulbs have flat, black scales. Usually on marshy sites in low areas, slopes in hill areas. Central counties and the Grand Prairie. May-August.

H. liriosme, Spider Lily, which is nearly identical, is a more southern species that is also found on the Grand Prairie. It has an earlier, shorter blooming period than *H. caroliniana*.

A

B

C

D

A YELLOW STAR GRASS   *Hypoxis hirsuta*

The bright yellow flowers are up to ³/₄ inch (18 mm) wide and often bloom when the
plant is only a few inches (cm) high. A hairy, grasslike plant that is usually about 1 foot
(30 cm) high when fully grown. The seeds are eaten by quail. Open woods, prairies,
glades, on a variety of soils. Nearly statewide. May-August.

B SPRING STAR-FLOWER   *Ipheion uniflorum*

The white, pale pink or light blue flowers are about 1 inch (2.5 cm) wide with
triangular "petals" which form a starlike shape. This species is only a few inches tall
with wide, grasslike leaves. Grows in isolated clumps and in carpets that cover large
areas. The main blooming period is over before lawn-mowing time. A cultivated
species that often escapes. These plants have a garliclike odor when bruised. Gardens,
lawns, especially around older homes, cemeteries. Scattered counties in eastern and
central Arkansas. March-April.

   Zephranthes candida, White Rain-lily, has escaped cultivation in several southern
counties. It is about 1 foot (30 cm) tall with white, slender petals nearly 1 inch (2.5 cm)
long. The leaves are ¹/₄ inch (6 mm) wide and there is one flower per stalk.

IRIS FAMILY (Iridaceae)

C PURPLE PLEAT-LEAF, PINEWOODS LILY   *Alophia drummondii*

The flower is 1¹/₂ inches (3.8 cm) wide and colored with shades of light to dark purple.
The light-colored center has purplish dots. The sepals are spreading and the petals are
cupped. Each flower lasts only a day. A small plant with leaves up to 1¹/₂ feet (45 cm)
long and 1 inch (2.5 cm) wide with distinct veins. Pinelands, sandy soils. Recorded in
3 southern counties: Calhoun, Miller and Union. May-June.

D BLACKBERRY LILY   *Belamcanda chinensis*

A flat, symmetrical, orange flower with reddish or crimson spots on the "petals. " Each
bloom is about 2 inches (5 cm) wide and lasts only one day. Although the flower is
lilylike, this plant is in the Iris Family and has only three stamens (lilies have 6). The
fruit is a capsule that opens to expose a compact group of shiny, round, black seeds
resembling a blackberry. The leaves are flat, about 1 foot (30 cm) or less in length and
1 inch (2.5 cm) wide. This species is a perennial about 2-3 feet (60-90 cm) tall and is
easily grown from seed or roots. An alien from Asia that has been widely cultivated.
Rocky, open or glade areas on well-drained soils. Ozark and Ouachita Mountain
Region counties, also Arkansas County. Summer.

A

B

C

D

Seven species of wild iris are known to occur in Arkansas.

A SHORT-STEMMED IRIS, LAMANCE IRIS   *Iris brevicaulis*

The flowers are 4-5 inches (10-12.5 cm) wide, deep blue to purple and not crested. They are not terminal as are those of most other irises. A 6-sided capsule is produced. This species is about 2 feet (60 cm) tall with zig-zag, often reclining stems. Wet areas, marshes, near streams and lakes. Known from 6 counties: Arkansas, Ashley, Clark, Saline, Washington and Benton. April-May.

B CRESTED IRIS   *Iris cristata*

The violet-blue to nearly white flowers have crested or bearded sepals. These have yellow ridges bordered with white. The flower is large in proportion to the plant size and measures $2\frac{1}{2}$ inches (6.3 cm) wide. There are 1-2 flowers per plant. A non-fragrant species. This is a short species usually less than 1 foot (30 cm) tall. The rhizomes have thick, scaly segments with slender, stringlike connections. Rocky or sandy soil along streams, hillsides, bottom of slopes. Well distributed in the Ozark and Ouachita Mountain regions. April-May.

C COPPER IRIS, RED IRIS   *Iris fulva*

The flowers are copper-red with variations. The petals and sepals are somewhat flattened and the flower is about $2\frac{1}{2}$ inches (6.3 cm) wide. These plants are up to 4 feet (1.2 meters) high with leaves 3 feet (1 meter) long that are basal. Marshes, swamps, wet areas, streams. Eastern and southern counties. April-May.

D DWARF IRIS   *Iris verna*

A small, fragrant iris with more yellow in the petals than Crested Iris. The petals and sepals are purplish and the sepals are not crested. The plants are short, with narrow leaves. Moist or dry sites. Montgomery, Ouachita, Polk and Saline counties in the Ouachita Mountain Region. A rare iris in Arkansas. April-May.

A

B

C

D

A   SOUTHERN BLUE FLAG   *Iris virginica*

Several color variations occur with the white, blue, violet or purple tones varying. The most common color combination is as shown. The flowers are about 3 inches (7.5 cm) wide. The foliage is typical of this genus and is sometimes reclining. The flower stalks reach 3 feet (1 meter) in height. Wet areas, swamps, marshes, bogs, spring branches, shallow areas in lakes. Nearly statewide, but more common in the southern counties. April- May.

I.pseudacorus, Yellow Flag, is a European species that has escaped from cultivation in several southern states. It is a tall species 3-4 feet (1-1.2 meters) high with large, bright yellow flowers 3-4 inches (7.5-10 cm) wide. Grows in wet, swampy areas, along rivers, edges of lakes. Has been discovered in several central Arkansas counties, also Washington. April-May. See page 270.

B   CELESTIAL LILY   *Nemastylis geminiflora*

A delicate light blue or blue-violet flower that opens in the morning and soon fades. The flowers often occur in pairs and are up to 2^1/$_2$ inches (6.3 cm) wide. Long narrow leaves clasp the stem and are about 1 foot (30 cm) tall. A variety of sites: glades, rocky areas, limestone soils, occasionally pinelands. A few southwestern counties, Arkansas and Jefferson counties in the Delta Region; eastern counties in the Ozark Region. Not commonly found. April-May.

N. Nuttallii, Celestial Lily, is a similar species that occurs in a few northern counties. It has been collected recently in Jefferson County.

C   BLUE-EYED GRASS   *Sisyrinchium* spp.

The blue flowers, sometimes white, are about ^{1}/$_2$ inch (13 mm) wide and have yellow centers and yellow stamens. The petals and sepals are tipped with small bristles. The flower stalks are taller than the leaves or sometimes the flowers occur about mid- way on the plants. The flowers emerge from grasslike bracts. The grasslike plants are about 1 foot (30 cm) tall, with narrow leaves, and grow in clumps. Individual species are very difficult to identify; 8 have been collected in Arkansas. There are both perennials and annuals. A wide variety of sites. Statewide. April-June.

D   BLUE-EYED GRASS   * *Sisyrinchium exile*

The yellowish to nearly white flowers are ^{1}/$_2$ inch (13 mm) wide with brown or purplish viens. A short plant that has foliage similar to that of other species of blue-eyed grass. An annual. Sandy soils. A few south-central counties and Polk County are the presently recorded locations. April-June.

A

B

C

D

ARROWROOT FAMILY (Marantaceae)

Only one species from this family occurs in Arkansas.

A   POWDERY THALIA, THALIA   *Thalia dealbata*

The purplish flowers are in a terminal, spreading inflorescence on a long stalk above the leaves. There is a large, sickle-shaped bract below the inflorescence in early stages of bloom. Each flower is about ³/₄ inch (18 mm) wide. The plants are often 6 feet (1. 8 meters) or more in height, with large, oval leaves. All parts of this species are covered with a white powdery coating (glaucous). Wet ditches, edges of bodies of water. Mainly in eastern and northeastern counties in the Delta Region, also Hempstead and Nevada counties. June- October.

ORCHID FAMILY (Orchidaceae)

Forty orchids are known from within the boundaries of the state. All are treated here, however, the 11 species and varieties of ladies' tresses are treated as a group.

B   PUTTY ROOT, ADAM-AND-EVE   *Aplectrum hyemale*

The greenish or yellowish flowers have a white lip marked with purple. The sepals and petals are about ¹/₂ inch (13 mm) long and more regular in shape than those of most orchid flowers. The flower stalk is 1-1¹/₂ feet (30-45 cm) tall. The single large, oval leaf develops during the fall, usually in October, and persists throughout the winter. About the time of the appearance of the flower stalk the leaf withers. Hill areas where moisture and fertility are good. Recorded in Garland, Logan, Madison, Newton, Pope and Stone counties, but should occur in several other hill counties. May-June.

C   OKLAHOMA GRASS-PINK   * *Calopogon oklahomensis*

The fragrant, rose-pink to nearly white blossoms have spreading, recurved lateral sepals. The uppermost lip is bearded and concave. In Rose Pogonia the bearded lip is below. The flower buds are grooved in this grass- pink. Several flowers are in bloom at the same time. The flower is about 1¹/₂ inches (3.8 cm) wide. The single, grasslike leaf sheaths the flower stalk and grows as high or higher than the flowers, the plants are about 1 foot (30 cm) tall. Common in some areas. Prairies, bogs in open areas, often on sandy soils. The Grand Prairie and a few other scattered locations. April-July.

    C. tuberosus, Grass-pink, is a larger plant with larger flowers. The flowers open in succession and the flower buds are not grooved. The leaf is not as high as the inflorescence. The sepals are straight and the flowers are not fragrant. Wet pine woodlands. Saline County and possibly surrounding areas. Late May-July.

D   SPRING CORAL ROOT   *Corallorhiza wisteriana*

The flowers are brown or reddish-brown with a white lip that is crinkled and spotted with crimson or purple dots. The flowers last only a few hours. They are about ¹/₄ inch (6mm) wide and ¹/₂ to ³/₄ inch (13-18 mm) long. As the plants age the stems and fruits turn brown. The stems and the alternate, scalelike leaves are light brown to slightly purplish. There is no bulb at the base of this plant. Coral roots lack pigment and "feed" upon organic matter in the soil (saprophytic). The plants are 4 inches (10 cm) to 1 foot (30 cm) tall. Dry woodlands in leaf mold. Scattered over most of the state. March-June.

    C. odontorhiza, Late Coral Root, has smaller flowers and a narrower lip. There is a small bulb at the base of the plant and the blooming period is August-October. Recorded in northcentral and 2 southwestern counties.

A

B

C

D

A   LARGE YELLOW LADY'S-SLIPPER   *Cypripedium parviflorum* var. *pubescens*

The slipper or lip is a rich yellow and is sometimes reduced in size. The flowers measure 2 inches (5 cm) or more in length and are carried at the ends of the upright stalks, one or two to each plant. The twisted lateral petals are yellowish, spotted with brown or reddish brown. The 3-5 oval leaves have prominent, parallel veins, are often pointed and are somewhat hairy, especially at the nodes. The plants are 2-2½ feet (60-75 cm) high. Most often found on rich, moist sites in woodlands, especially on slopes. Mainly in the western and northern parts of the state and on Crowley's Ridge. April-June.

C. kentuckiense, Kentucky Lady's-slipper, has recently been determined to be the most common of the state's yellow lady's-slippers. It occurs throughout the range given for *C. pubescens* and many of the plants formerly thought to be this species are actually *C. kentuckiense*. It is a large plant up to 3 feet (1 meter) tall with a pale, deep, lip ("slipper") that barely extends past its opening. Usually one flower per plant, occasionally two, pedicels long, up to 8 inches (10 cm). Blooms later than our other yellow lady's-slippers and has the largest flowers. *C. parviflorum* var. *parviflorum,* Small Yellow Lady's-slipper, is usually described as not over 1 foot (30 cm) high with flowers 1 inch (2.5 cm) or less in length and fragrant. The petals are more twisted than those of Large Yellow Lady's-slipper and burgundy to very dark brown. The plant is only slightly hairy.

B   SHOWY LADY'S-SLIPPER   *Cypripedium reginae*

This large-flowered species with a pink "slipper" and white sepals presently is known only from Stone County where possibly the last small colony of the species in the state was found by the late Richard Davis in 1981. It formerly grew on the other sites in Stone and Benton Counties.

C   SHOWY ORCHIS   *Galearis spectabilis (=Orchis spectabilis)*

The two-colored flower is about 1 inch (2.5 cm) long with a rich lavender hood and white lower lip. All white or all purplish flowers sometimes occur. The flowers are fragrant and are carried on a short stalk. The plants are 6-12 inches (15-30 cm) high and smooth. Two large leaves surround the stalk at ground level and spread outward. This is the only species of the genus *Orchis* (recently renamed *Galearis*) in the state. Fertile woodland soils, sometimes in disturbed areas. Ozark Region counties and Crowley's Ridge. April-June.

D   RATTLESNAKE PLANTAIN   *Goodyera pubescens*

The small white flowers are ¼ - ½ inch (6-13 mm) long and in a spike at the top of a hairy stalk. The upper sepal and two petals form a hood and the lip is saclike. The leaves are deep green to bluish-green with white veins creating the "rattlesnake" pattern. They fade soon after blooming to be replaced by leaves that persist until the next blooming period. The plants grow to about 18 inches (45 cm) high. Dry or moist sites in woodlands, openings, slopes. A few Ozark Region counties and Polk County. Common in a few local areas. August-September.

A

B

C

D

A   CRESTED CORAL ROOT   *Hexalectris spicata*

The flesh-colored flowers are $^3/_4$ inches (18 mm) long or longer and slightly tinged with orange. The sepals are longer than the petals and streaked. The flowering portion of the stalk is up to 1 foot (30 cm) long. The stems are brownish with purplish, sheathing bracts. There are sometimes several stems per plant. These grow to $2^1/_2$ feet (75 cm) high. The plants are saprophytic. Moist woodlands. Recorded in 3-4 northern counties. Reported from Hempstead and Pulaski counties. July-August.

B   LARGE WHORLED POGONIA   *Isotria verticillata*

The yellowish-green flowers above a whorl of 5-6 leaves average about $1^1/_2$ inches (3.8 cm) long. The spreading sepals are purplish. The flowers begin to bloom before the leaves are fully developed. The plants often remain inactive for periods of several years. This species often occurs in colonies several feet in width. The plants are 6-12 inches (15-30 cm) tall. Acid woods, slopes, near springs and damp ground, thickets, shady woodlands. Lower two-thirds of the state. April-May.

C   LARGE TWAYBLADE, LILY TWAYBLADE   *Liparis lilifolia*

The $^3/_4$ inch (18 mm) long flowers have a maroon or reddish-brown lip, 3 narrow green sepals and 2 threadlike maroon lateral petals. The plant is about 10 inches (25 cm) high when in flower. Two shiny, smooth leaves surround the single flower stalk at ground level. Rich woodland soils of slopes, moist streambanks, mossy areas, sometimes cut-over areas. Mainly in northcentral counties, also Benton County. May-July.

     L. loeslii, Loesel's Twayblade, has recently been discovered near the Garland-Montgomery County line. Vegetatively it is similar to the above species but the flowers are smaller, fewer and more widely spaced along the upper stem. The lip is much less noticeable and the drooping lateral petals are much shortened. Grows in wet situations.

D   SOUTHERN TWAYBLADE   *Listera australis*

The flowers are either reddish-brown on brown stalks or yellowish, on light-colored stalks. The lower lip is divided into two relatively long segments which point downward. The entire flower is slightly over $^1/_3$ inch (8 mm) long. The two opposite, sessile leaves are about $^3/_4$ inch (18 mm) long and oval on stalks about 1 foot (30 cm) long. Moist woodlands, pinelands with humus. Recorded in Bradley, Columbia, Jefferson, Pike and Union counties, however, these small, slender plants have probably been overlooked in other locations. March-May.

A

B

C

D

A   GREEN ADDERS' MOUTH   *Malaxis unifolia*

The very small greenish to greenish-white flowers are closely grouped on a slender stem. There is a 2-lobed lip and threadlike side petals. A single oval leaf partly surrounds the stalk about midway. It measures 3-4 inches (7.5- 10 cm) long on a stalk 10 inches (25 cm) or less in height. An easily overlooked species. Rich, moist woodland soils, shady areas. Western Arkansas, also Clay and Greene counties, Ashley, Jefferson, Saline and Union counties. April-May.

The genus *Platanthera* (=*Habenaria*) contains 7 species that are known to be present in the state at this time. None of these are very common. They are often found in damp, wooded areas and near springs. Most of the species have only a few leaves.

B   YELLOW FRINGED ORCHID   *Platanthera ciliaris*

The flower is usually a light orange color in spite of the common name. Each flower has prominent fringes and a spur that is longer than the flower. The entire flower measures about $1\frac{1}{2}$ inches (3.8 cm) long. The inflorescence averages 3-5 inches (7.5-12.5 cm) in length. The lower leaves are long, slender and clasping. The plant is 1-3 feet (30-90 cm) tall. Moist or dry sites in sandy, acid soils, near springs, low pineland areas, occasionally rocky soils or slopes. Sometimes in disturbed soils of pipelines, roadways, etc. Primarily in Ouachita Mountain and Gulf Coastal Plain Region counties. July-August.

C   GREEN WOOD ORCHID   *Platanthera clavellata*

The whitish flowers have a greenish cast and are $\frac{1}{4}$ inch (6 mm) wide. There is a short, blunt lip with 3 small rounded lobes that are not fringed and short spurs. Pollination is by mosquitoes and possibly other small insects. There is a large clasping leaf, low on the stalk of flowering plants. The stem leaves are progressively smaller up the stalk. Young or non-blooming plants have only the single large leaf. The plants are 1- $1\frac{1}{2}$ feet (30-45 cm) tall when in bloom. Moist woodlands, acid ground near springs, seepy ground, often in shady thickets or near ferns. A few central counties, Hempstead, Pike, Polk and Union counties, also Clay and Greene counties. June-July.

D   CRESTED FRINGED ORCHID   *Platanthera cristata*

Somewhat similar to the Yellow Fringed Orchid but with smaller flowers. The fringes are short and the spur is shorter than the flower. The flowers are yellow. Boggy areas, sandy moist sites, often in association with ferns. Recorded in Grant, Jefferson, Pulaski, Saline and Union counties. June-August.

P. nivea, Snowy Orchid, was reported before the turn of the century from the Grand Prairie. The flowers are small and white with the lip uppermost. There is a long, slightly curved spur that is horizontal with an upturned end.

A

B

D

C

A PALE GREEN ORCHID   *Platanthera flava*

The uniformly green flowers blend with the green color of other vegetation. There is a flat lip with a small lobe on each side near the base. Narrow bracts hang behind the flowers, which have rounded petals. The flowers are less than $1/2$ inch (13 mm) wide. The leaves are smooth, dark green and glossy on the upper surface. The plants are 1-2 feet (30-60 cm) high. Damp, shady woods, spring bogs, low wet areas. Ashley, Conway, Faulkner, St. Francis and Union counties are recorded locations. Recently transplanted to one other central county. June-July,

B RAGGED ORCHID   *Platanthera lacera*

The flowers are usually greenish with white fringes but the coloration varies, including cream or whitish shades. They are less than 1 inch (2.5 cm) long with several slender fringes on the 3-parted lower lip. The amount of fringe varies from plant to plant. The spur is about the same length as the flower. Erect, slender leaves are about 8 inches (20 cm) long on the lower part of the plant. The leaves on the stalk are small. Flowering plants are about 2 feet (60 cm) high. Prairies, open or thin woods, usually in damp ground. Grand Prairie, western and northwestern counties, also Drew and Pulaski counties. May or June into summer.

C PURPLE FRINGELESS ORCHID   *Platanthera peramoena*

A pinkish-lavender to reddish-purple flower with a 3-parted lip. The middle part of the lip is slightly notched. The flowers are nearly 1 inch (2.5 cm) long. The leaves are mainly basal and sheath the stem. A tall species that may grow to more than 3 feet (1 meter) high. Moist woods, often in shady groves of trees. Recorded in 3 central and 3 northeastern counties. Not often found. May-August.

D WATER-SPIDER ORCHID   *Habenaria repens*

The small greenish flowers are spiderlike, with the lip cleft into 3 narrow lobes, and measure about $1/2$ inch (13 mm) wide. This is a leafy species with some leaves 1 foot (30 cm) long. The plants grow to 2 feet (60 cm) tall. An aquatic orchid found in muddy areas near lakes or on floating logs or debris. Recorded in only 3 scattered counties at this time: Saline, Hempstead and Union. August-October.

A

B

C

D

A ROSE POGONIA, SNAKE-MOUTH   *Pogonia ophioglossoides*

The rose-colored petals and sepals are similarly shaped. The lip at the bottom of the flower is fringed and bearded with yellowish bristles. There is one flower per plant, about 1½ inches (3- 8 cm) long. One leaf is located about mid-way up the stalk at flowering time, oval or long-oval in shape. Plants are up to 18 inches (45 cm) tall. Damp, open or shady woods, prairies, meadows, other low, damp areas. Rare, known from only two counties in the central part of the state and Fulton County. May-July.

Cleistes divaricata, Spreading Pogonia, Rosebud Orchid, may possibly occur in extreme south Arkansas. It is a tall plant, up to 2½ feet (75 cm) high, with a single leaf. The flower is pink to light pink with 3 spreading, slender, dark-colored sepals and a crested lower lip. The flower is carried at the top of the stalk in a nodding position and is up to 3 inches (7.5 cm) long. The blooming period is May-July.

B LADIES' TRESSES   *Spiranthes spp.*

Small white blossoms spiral up the top part of the stalk. Basal, grasslike leaves. The height varies among the species. Various sites, from rocky hillsides to moist woods, prairies, vacant lots, roadsides and highway medians. Not uncommon but often overlooked. Nearly statewide. Summer-fall.

C CRANE-FLY ORCHID   *Tipularia discolor*

The flowers appear a light brown or tan, but close examination at full bloom will reveal green and purple tints. A slender, delicate plant easily passed by because it blends with the color of the ground. A slender spur extends back from the drooping flower which is about ½ inch (13 mm) wide. There is a single large leaf that is purplish underneath with prominent veins. It is oval, appears in the fall and withers in the spring before the flower stalk puts up. The stalk is leafless and usually less than 2 feet (60 cm) tall. Wet or dry sites in woodlands, slopes with open ground cover. Often in beech or other hardwood forests. Mainly in the central and southwestern counties and on Crowley's Ridge. July-September.

D NODDING POGONIA   *Triphora trianthophora*

The light pink or white flowers have 3 greenish streaks on the upper lip. The upper 2 petals form a hood. Often bears 3 blossoms, which has led to another common name - "Three Birds." The blossoms last only a short time and the plants may bloom only once in several years. The flowers are about ¾ inch (18 mm) long. A small plant, seldom over 10 inches (25 cm) high. with short, oval leaves that partly surround the stem. In humus of hardwood forests. Scattered counties in the western half of the state. July-September.

A

B

C

D

DICOTYLEDONS

LIZARD'S-TAIL FAMILY (Saururaceae)

A single species from this family occurs in Arkansas.

A   LIZARD'S-TAIL   *Saururus cernuus*

The flowers appear white because of the white stamens. The "tail" or flower spike
bearing the tiny, fragrant flowers is 4-8 inches (10-20 cm) Iong. There are no petals or
sepals. The heart-shaped leaves are 4-6 inches (10-15 cm) long. This plant often occurs
in thick stands. Damp ground or shallow water. Open or shaded sites. Widespread but
not recorded in some western counties. June-August,

SANDALWOOD FAMILY (Santalaceae)

The family is represented by a single species in this state.

B   BASTARD TOADFLAX   *Comandra umbellata*
Small, white or greenish- white flowers remain in a semi-closed position in close
groups at the tops of the plants. The leaves are oblong and average about 1 inch (2.5
cm) in length with pale undersides. The plants grow to about 16 inches (40 cm) high.
Open woods and glades. Northern counties and a few eastern counties. April-June.

BIRTHWORT FAMILY (Aristolochiaceae)

C   PIPE VINE, DUTCHMAN'S PIPE   *Arisiolochia tomentosa*

Pale tan or yellowish flowers with a purple orifice (mouth) are about $1^1/_2$ inches (3.8
cm) long and are borne in the leaf axils, either singly or in pairs. This species is a high
climbing vine with large, downy, heart-shaped leaves. Stream and river banks, damp
woods with fertile soil. Mainly in the western half of the state. April- May.

   *A. serpentari*a, Virginia Snakeroot, has smaller flowers that are about $^1/_2$ inch (13 mm)
long and are borne on the lower branches of the small, erect plants. The leaves are
narrowly heart-shaped. Occurs over most of the state but not reported from Delta
Region counties.

D   WILD GINGER   *Asarum canadense*

This flower is without petals. The 3, pointed calyx lobes are a rich reddish-brown. The
flowers are about $^3/_4$ inch (18mm) long and arise from the leaf axils. This is a low,
creeping species with the flowers usually hidden in the ground cover. The leaves are a
rounded heart-shape and shiny on the upper side. The roots are sometimes used as a
ginger flavoring. Fertile woodland soils. Often found with Jack- in-the-pulpit, trout
lilies, bloodroot, etc. Mainly in northwestern Arkansas and on Crowley's Ridge.
April-May

A

B

C

D

SMARTWEED OR BUCKWHEAT FAMILY (Polygonaceae)

A   UMBRELLA PLANT   *Eriogonum longifolium*

Small, greenish-white flowers are scattered over the angular, fuzzy stems in the top part of the plant. The flower stems somewhat resemble the ribs of an umbrella. These plants often grow 5-6 feet (1.5-1.8 meters) high. The leaves are basal, velvet-gray underneath, long and slender in shape around the upright stalk. Only a few small leaves occur on the upper part of the stalk. Dry roadbanks, ledges, woodland openings, upland areas. Mainly in Ouachita Mountain Region and eastern Ozark Region counties. June-July.

B   JOINTWEED   *Polygonella americana*

Small, fringed, white flowers are in clusters at right angles to each other. Thick groups of small pointed leaves on the branching stems give a compact, shrubby appearance. The plants are usually less than 2 feet (60 cm) high on bluffs and cliffs, higher on more moist sites. Rocky hillsides, bluffs, open rocky areas, along streams. Northcentral and southwestern counties are the main reported locations. August-October.

The genus *Polygonum* (smartweeds) contains 19 recorded species in the state. The seeds are an important waterfowl and game bird food source.

C   WATER SMARTWEED   * *Polygonum coccineum*

The flower spike is made up of many small pink to red flowers and is 3-5 inches (7.5-12.5 cm) long. The vegetation is rank growing and the stalks may be reclining or erect reaching 3 feet (1 meter) in length. The leaves of smartweeds have a sharp or "smart" taste. The knotty stem-joints are a trademark of the genus. Swamps, ditches, shallow wet areas. Over most of the state in scattered locations. Variable blooming period - late spring into summer.

D   PINKWEED, PENNSYLVANIA SMARTWEED   *Polygonim pensylvanicum*

The pink flowers and reddish buds are on erect stalks up to 4 feet (1.2 meters) high. The stamens and the styles usually do not protrude from the calyx. The upper stems have tiny glands. The leaves are slender on reddish steins. The seeds are eaten by quail, waterfowl and doves. Wet areas. Nearly statewide but more common in the northern two-thirds. June-September.

P. sagittatum, Arrow-leaved Tear-thumb, has short white flower heads scattered over the top part of the plants, which are usually in thick, tangled masses on low ground. The leaves are arrowhead-shaped and parallel to the stem of the plant. They are narrow and light green in color. There are very strong, recurved spines on the stems and underside of the midrib of the leaf. Low areas. Scattered occurrence. June-October.

A

B

C

D

AMARANTH FAMILY (Amaranthaceae)

A COTTONWEED   *Froelichia floridana*

The somewhat pyramid-shaped spikes are whitish and cottonlike. Each is about 1-2 inches (2.5-5 cm) long. The plants are erect and grow to about 5 feet (1.5 meters) high. Dry, sandy soils. Reported from counties in the eastern two-thirds of the state. June-October.

F. gracilis, Cottonweed, is a smaller species than the above that occurs over the northern two-thirds of the state. May-September. *Alternanthera philoxeroides*, Alligator Weed, has trailing stems that form mats in wet areas. The long, bare flower stalks are erect with white, compact, burlike flower heads and arise from the axils of the opposite leaves. The flower stalks are up to 3 inches (7.5 cm) long with flower heads about ½ inch (13 mm) across. Found mainly in southeastern counties. Blooms from April to October.

FOUR-O-CLOCK FAMILY (Nyctaginaceae)

B WILD FOUR-O'CLOCK   *Mirabilis nyctaginea*

Small, pink to purplish-pink flowers are in the top part of the plants or near the ends of the branches in partial whorls and are set in 5-lobed cups. The leaves are indented or slightly heart- shaped at the base. The plants may grow to 3 feet (1 meter) high or higher with branching stems. Along railroads, roadsides, idle land. Central and northern counties, Little River and Hempstead counties. May-June.

M. albida, White Four O'Clock, has small flowers that soon fade to leave the flat, greenish- white calyx with the brownish seeds adhering. This plant is usually found in woodland openings in the western two-thirds of the state and blooms during May-August.

POKEWEED FAMILY (Phytolaccaceae)

One member of the family occurs in Arkansas.

C POKEWEED   *Phytolacca americana*

The small, white flowers are in a tapering raceme. Purple to black berries with a staining juice are used as a food coloring and in dyes. The berries and seeds are eaten by song and game birds. The plants are eaten by deer. The stems are branching and purplish near the ends. The leaves of young plants, "poke salad," are eaten by some people in the spring months. Grows well on disturbed ground, roadsides, ditch banks, lots, cutover or burned woodlands. Statewide. June- October.

PURSLANE FAMILY (Portulacaceae)

D SPRING BEAUTY   *Claytonia virginica*

The flowers are pink or white with pink to reddish veins in the petals; occasionally all white flowers occur. They measure ½ inch (13 mm) across. These plants grow singly or in clumps with slender, grasslike leaves. Before flowering occurs the leaves are purplish. This is one of the earliest lawn flowers. Was in bloom February 5, 1984 in Little Rock after one of the most severe winters on record. Browsed by deer in spring months. Lawns, lots, open woods, open areas. Statewide. February-May.

C. caroliniana, Carolina Spring Beauty, is found in only 4 counties: Cleburne, Van Buren, Faulkner and Washington. It has much broader leaves than those of *C. virginica* and they are often nearly heart-shaped. March-April.

A

B

C

D

A FAME FLOWER, ROCK PINK   *Talinum calycinum*

The colorful, deep red or wine-red flowers about ³/₄ inch (18 mm) wide are on slender leafless stalks. There are up to 25 or more stamens. Each flower is open for only a few hours. Succulent, basal leaves are shaped like small weiners. Rocky areas, cedar glades. Well distributed in the Ozark and Ouachita Mountain regions. May-July.

 T. parviflorum, Fame Flower, Rock Pink, is somewhat more southern in distribution with pink flowers and only 5-6 stamens. Later blooming.

PINK OR CARNATION FAMILY (Caryophyllaceae)

B CORN COCKLE   *Agrostemma githago*

The showy, pink to reddish flowers are 1 inch (2.5 cm) wide or wider with long pointed sepals protruding past the petals. The plants stand about 2 feet (60 cm) high and are hairy. A native of Europe that is sometimes weedy in corn fields or other cultivated crops. Fields, roadsides, idle land. Ozark Region and a few northern Delta Region counties. June-September.

C SANDWORT   *Arenaria patula*

Small white flowers about ¹/₄ inch (6 mm) wide are carried on slender stems having small glands. The stems may reach 6-8 inches (15-20 cm) in height. Basal leaves form mats of cedarlike foliage with linear, needlelike leaves that are opposite. An annual plant. Sandy or light soils. Variable sites over most of the state. April-June,

D DEPTFORD PINK   *Dianthus armeria*

The pink to reddish flowers with small white dots on the petals occur mainly in the top part of the plants and are about ¹/₂ inch (13 mm) wide. The stems are stiff and upright with narrow, pointed leaves. Plants are up to 2 feet (60 cm) tall. A native of Europe. Roadsides, dry fields, open woods, glades. Hill counties, especially in northern Arkansas. May-August.

A

B

C

D

A BOUNCING BET, SOAPWORT   *Saponaria officinalis*

The white, pink or lavender blooms are near the tops of the plants. The petals often curl back, are slightly notched and the flower is about 1 inch (2.5 cm) wide. The plants sometimes form large colonies. The juice when mixed with water will form a lather. Native of Europe. Near streams or other damp areas, also along roads and railroads. More common in northern Arkansas, scattered in southern counties. June-September.

Lychnis alba, White Campion, has white to pinkish, fragrant flowers with an enlarged calyx that resemble those of Bouncing Bet. The male flowers have 10 stamens. The female flowers have 5 protruding styles. A native of Europe with downy or hairy opposite leaves. Reported from Benton and Washington counties. May-September.

B STARRY CAMPION   *Silene stellata*

The white flowers with fringed petals are about 1 inch (2.5 cm) wide. There are long stamens and an enlarged, rounded calyx. The lanceolate leaves are in whorls of 4 on the stalks. The stems are sticky. The plants average 2-3 feet (60-90 cm) high. Slopes, along streams, woodlands. Hill areas in northern and western Arkansas. June-August.

S. ovata is a white flowered species also, but with petals deeply cut into many slender lobes. The long slender stamens stand straight out from the center of the flower and are as long as the petals. The plants may reach 4 feet (1. 2 meters) in height. This species has been recorded in Cleburne, Pope, Stone and Benton counties. August- November.

C FIRE PINK   *Silene virginica*

The bright red flowers are up to 1½ inches (3.8 cm) wide with yellow stamens. The ends of the petals are notched into two short pointed lobes. The face of the petals is grooved. The stems are somewhat sticky, hairy and up to 2 feet (60 cm) tall. The leaves are smooth, opposite, and spatulate. Slopes, open woods, roadsides. Widely distributed in all Ozark and Ouachita Mountain Region counties, also a few other counties. April-June.

D ROYAL CATCHFLY   *Silene regia*

This species has bright red flowers and may grow to 5 feet (1.5 meters) high. The stems are usually smooth but the leaves may be pubescent. The flowers are up to 2 inches (5 cm) in width with narrow, unnotched or slightly notched petals. The face of the petals is smooth. The leaves are broad, opposite, pointed, and rounded or clasping at the base. Reported in 5 northern counties and Hot Spring County. Has been reported from most of the counties in the Ozark Region of southern Missouri. May-September.

A

B

C

D

WATER LILY FAMILY (Nymphaeaceae)

A   WATER-SHIELD   *Brasenia schreberi*

The reddish-purple flowers are about 1 inch (2.5 cm) long. Underwater parts are covered with a clear, jellylike substance. Leaves are 3-4 inches (7.5- 10 cm) long and oval. Lakes, ponds, ditches. Not common. Found mainly in south Arkansas. April-June.

B   YONCAPIN, AMERICAN LOTUS   *Nelumbo lutea*

The large yellow flowers are often 8 inches (20 cm) across. Acornlike seeds are borne in a nodding receptable that resembles a shower head. The large circular leaves often measure 2 feet (60 cm) across. They shed water as if waxed and may cover large areas often becoming a problem to fishermen and boaters. Indians ate the roots, young shoots and seeds. Lakes, ponds, canals, ditches, reservoirs where there is a mud bottom. Statewide. Late summer months.

C   YELLOW POND LILY   ** Nuphar luteum*

Round, yellow flowers with greenish-yellow sepals are about $1\frac{1}{2}$ inches (3.8 cm) in diameter. There is a thick disc above the ovary. The leaves are about 1 foot (30 cm) in diameter. This plant has large rhizomes. Aquatic animals and waterfowl feed upon the plants and seeds. Nearly all types of water areas including streams, lakes, and bayous. Scattered over the state. April-October.

D   FRAGRANT WATER LILY   *Nymphaea odorata*

The large white blossoms have 4 sepals, many petals and numerous yellow stamens. The leaves are circular with a notch at the base and are purple underneath. Ponds and lakes. Statewide. April-August.

A

B

C

D

CROWFOOT OR BUTTERCUP FAMILY (Ranunculaceae)

A WHITE BANEBERRY, DOLL'S-EYES ** Actaea pachypoda*

Small white flowers with narrow petals and prominent stamens are in a dense raceme above the leaves. The fruits are white berries with a black scar or "pupil" creating the resemblance to a doll's eye. The compound leaves are sharply toothed. A perennial plant that grows to 3 feet (1 meter) high. Rich woods. Crowley's Ridge and westcentral counties. April-May.

B ANEMONE *Anemone berlandieri*

The white or pinkish, poppylike flowers have greenish or yellowish stamens and about 10 petallike sepals - no petals. The basal leaves are divided into three segments having lobes. If stem leaves are present they are divided into slender, fingerlike lobes. Open ground, sandy areas, prairies. Southwestern counties, scattered in a few Ozark and Ouachita Mountain Region counties. March-April.

    A. caroliniana, Carolina Anemone, has a white, poppylike flower with orange stamens. The backside of the numerous sepals (no petals) is tinted with lavender. Flowers are about 1$\frac{1}{2}$ inches (3.8 cm) wide. There is one bloom on each of the 10-12 inch (25-30 cm) high stalks. The basal leaves are finely divided. A pair of leaves occurs midway up the stalk; these have a shredded appearance. Open areas, glades, prairies. Scattered in all regions, scarce in the Delta Region. March-April.

C THIMBLEWEED, TALL ANEMONE *Anemone virginiana*

The white to greenish-white flowers, without petals, have greenish centers and measure about 1 inch (2.5 cm) across. The center of the flower becomes thimble-shaped and may remain on the stalk for months. The plants grow to 3 feet (1 meter) high. The leaves are in 3 parts (trifoliate) with noticeably veined, toothed leaflets. Open woods, slopes, woodsides. Moist or dry sites. In most of the upland areas of the state. May-July.

D COLUMBINE *Aquilegia canadensis*

The red and yellow flowers have petals that extend into spurs with ball-shaped tips. The flowers are about 1$\frac{1}{2}$ inches (3.8 cm) long and hang face downward. The plants have spreading branches and are up to 2$\frac{1}{2}$ feet (75 cm) tall. The leaves are in 3-parted divisions. Rocky slopes, limestone ledges, shale, other soils. Mainly in the Ozark Region. April-June.

A

B

C

D

A BLACK SNAKEROOT   *Cimicifuga racemosa*

Very small white to yellowish-white flowers are in a long tapering raceme. There are numerous stamens but no petals. These plants reach 7-8 feet (2.1-2.4 meters) in height with large compound leaves that have 3 divisions. Moist woods, slopes, benches, valleys. Ozark Region. May-July.

The genus *Clematis* includes 8 recorded species in Arkansas. All are vines. Seven have attractive, vase-shaped flowers. In *C. virginiana,* Virgin's Bower, there are 4 white, petallike sepals at right angles to each other and fragrant flowers.

B LEATHER FLOWER   *Clematis crispa*

Considerable variation in the color of the flowers occurs including shades of white, violet or pink. The flowers are about 1 inch (2.5 cm) in length and are formed by the sepals. A climbing vine. Woodland edges and openings, roadsides, railroads, slopes and banks. Southeastern half of the state. May-August.

C LEATHER FLOWER   *Clematis pitcheri*

This species has lavender, vase-shaped flowers. The leaves are oval, usually with indented bases. The stems of the vines are reddish in color. Woodland edges, thickets. Collected from only a few counties in the Ozark and Ouachita Mountain regions. May-September.

   C viorna, Leather Flower, has bright red flowers and occurs in Ozark Region counties. Also Polk, Pulaski and Saline counties. See page 270.

The genus *Delphinium* is represented by 4 species in Arkansas.

D CAROLINA LARKSPUR, TALL LARKSPUR   *Delphinium carolinianum*

A tall plant up to 4 feet (1.2 meters) high with a long spike of deep blue, reddish-blue or whitish spurred flowers about $1\frac{1}{2}$ inches (3.8 cm) long. The leaves have very slender lobes. Open woods, slopes, ledges, roadsides. Nearly statewide except for parts of the Delta Region. May-July.

A

B

C

D

A   MOORE'S DELPHINIUM (ENDEMIC)   *Delphinium newtonianum*

The flowers are usually a sky-blue color but occasionally darker colors occur or rarely, white. This species can be recognized by the long pedicels on which one to several flowers occur. Plants are about 2 feet (60 cm) high with flowers around 1- 1$\frac{1}{4}$ inches (2.5-3 cm) long. This species was discovered by Dr. Dwight M. Moore in 1935 in Newton County and named after his father (Newton) and also after the name of the county. The species is endemic to Arkansas. Shady, moist woodlands. Recorded in Johnson, Newton, Pike, Pope and Searcy counties. June- July.

B   TRELEASE'S LARKSPUR   *Delphinium treleasei*

The purple flowers are on pedicels that are longer toward the bottom of the raceme. Pedicels are 1-3 inches (2.5-7.5 cm) long with one flower per pedicel. The leaf divisions are long and slender. Limestone or dolomite soils, usually on glades, road banks or other openings. Eight counties in extreme northwestern Arkansas is the presently recorded range. May-June.

C   DWARF LARKSPUR   *Delphinium tricorne*

A short species with white, blue, or blue-violet flowers. The leaves have palmate lobes that are wider than those of Carolina Larkspur or Trelease's Larkspur. Stream banks, rocky woods, valleys, slopes. Mainly in the Ozark and Ouachita Mountain regions. April-May.

D   ROUND-LOBED HEPATICA   *Hepatica nobilis* var. *obtusa*

The flowers are white or blue, sometimes pinkish, about $\frac{3}{4}$ inch (18 mm) wide and begin to appear earlier than the new leaves. There are 5-9 petallike sepals. The old leaves are liver- colored with 3 large, rounded lobes. The plants are only a few inches (cm) high. Ledges and slopes in woods or openings. Northern Ozark Region counties, also 3 Ouachita Mountain Region counties. February-April.

   H. nobilis var. *acuta*, Sharp-lobed Hepatica, is similar but the lobes of the leaves are sharp- pointed. Reported from Newton and Stone counties.

A

B

C

D

A   GOLDEN SEAL   *Hydrastis canadensis*

There are 3 greenish-white sepals and a circle of protruding stamens with yellowish tips. The flowers are about ¹/₂ inch (13 mm) wide. Dark red berries are produced. The young leaves are wrinkled and hairy. After flowering the leaves may grow to 10 inches (25 cm) across. The root is yellow with reported medicinal and dye uses. It has become rare in some areas because of extensive digging. Grows to about 1¹/₂ feet (45cm) tall. Rich, moist woodlands. Ozark Region uplands, Crowley's Ridge. April-May.

The genus *Ranunculus* includes the buttercups. A total of 18 species occurs in the state. Some of the species are difficult to identify.

B   BUTTERCUP   *Ranunculus spp.*

The bright yellow flowers often have shiny petals with rounded tips. There are numerous stamens and pistils. The leaves are deeply divided into slender or broad segments having lobes that are sharp-pointed or rounded. The seeds are often eaten by turkeys. Wet to dry areas in fields and woodlands. Statewide on all types of soils. May be found in bloom during any time of the year but mainly in spring and summer.

R. abortivus, Kidneyleaf Crowfoot, is an early-blooming species that may be recognized by its small, knoblike flowers with very small petals. The basal leaves are kidney-shaped or somewhat heart-shaped. Browsed by deer. Occurrence is statewide. March-May.

C   HISPID BUTTERCUP   *Ranunculus hispidus*

The petals are somewhat narrow and there may be more than 5. The seeds are not winged or flanged. The plants may be erect or reclining and have a stemy appearance. The stems are hairy. The leaves are divided into three segments with the end one stalked. Open or wooded sites. Western two-thirds of the state. March-June.

D   PURPLE MEADOW RUE   *Thalictrum dasycarpum*

The whitish flowers have tinges of purple or tan shading, especially near the tips of the petals. The leaves are finely hairy underneath with variously shaped segments. There are often three sharp lobes at the tips. The stems are sometimes purplish. The plants often reach 6 feet (1.8 meters) in height. Damp wooded slopes or open areas, fields. A few counties across the northern part of the state. May-July.

A

B

C

D

A   RUE ANEMONE   *Thalictrum thalictroides*

The flowers are about 1 inch (2.5 cm) wide and are usually arranged in whorls with each blossom on a separate pedicel. There are 5 to 11 sepals and many stamens and pistils. The sepals are white or pinkish. The upper leaves often are in whorls and each has 3 rounded lobes. This plant is easily cultivated. Woodlands, slopes, along streams. Found mainly in the Ozark and Ouachita Mountain regions. March-June.

Isopyrum biternatum, False Rue Anemone, is very similar except that the leaf tips are more lobed and the leaves arise from different levels on the stem. There are usually 5 of the petallike sepals. This species is more limited in distribution occurring mainly in the Ozark Region and a few south Arkansas counties. May occur in large, dense colonies. March-May.

BARBERRY FAMILY (Berberidaceae)

Two members of the family are found in Arkansas.

B   BLUE COHOSH   *Caulophyllum thalictroides*

The small flowers are in clusters. The usual color is greenish, sometimes brown. Dark blue berries are produced. The leaves are a "mitten" shape similar to those of Meadow Rue or Rue Anemone. Plants are up to 3 feet (1 meter) tall. Fertile woodland soils. Found in 3 northwestern counties: Benton, Logan and Stone. April-June.

C   MAY APPLE, MANDRAKE   *Podophyllum peltatum*

A white nodding flower about 2 inches (5 cm) wide grows from the fork of the two-leaved plants. It has 6-9 petals. The leaves are large, forming an easily recognized umbrella shape. Large colonies occur. Plants are 1-1$\frac{1}{2}$ feet (30-45 cm) high. Shady woodlands, thickets. Widespread over the state. March-May.

POPPY FAMILY (Papaveraceae)

D   PRICKLY POPPY   *Argemone albiflora*

The large flowers, 2 inches (5 cm) or more across, have thin white petals. Prickly, thistlelike grayish-green leaves and stems. Plants are often 3 feet (1 meter) tall or taller with a clear or white sap. An introduced species. Open fields, gravel bars, along streams, railroads. Northern Ozark Region counties, Little River County. May-August.

A

B

C

D

A   ORANGE POPPY, BLIND EYES   *Papaver dubium*

The orange or reddish flowers are slightly over 1 inch (2.5 cm) across with thin, delicate petals. Finely lobed or divided leaves have a feathery appearance. A cultivated plant that has escaped. Native of Europe. Roadsides, idle land. Northern counties in the Ozark Region. May-July.

B   BLOODROOT   *Sanguinaria canadensis*

The crisp, white, solitary flowers have 8 or more petals and are over 1 inch (2.5 cm) wide. Each flower lasts only a day. The rounded leaves have deeply cut lobes which curl around the stalk, especially when young. The roots have a bright red juice which was used by the Indians in making dye. The plants are up to 10 inches (25 cm) high. Rich woodlands, often along streams, slopes. Throughout the Ozark and Ouachita Mountain regions. Late February-April.

C   CELANDINE POPPY   *Stylophorum diphyllum*

Large, yellow to orange flowers have similarly colored stamens and 4 rounded petals. Thick, branching, low plants with yellow juice. There is a pair of opposite leaves below the flowers. Fertile woodland and strearnside sites. Recorded in Marion, Newton, Stone and Searcy counties. March-May.

FUMITORY FAMILY (Fumariaceae)

D   PALE CORYDALIS   *Corydalis flavula*

The pale yellow, drooping flowers are less than $1/2$ inch (13 mm) long with a small spur. They are attached to the stem near the center of the flower. The short plants often grow in thick colonies. Finely lobed leaves. Slopes, ledges, edges of woods and fields. Western Arkansas, Crowley's Ridge and other upland areas. March-May.

A

B

C

D

A DUTCHMAN'S BREECHES   *Dicentra cucullaria*

A thick row of the inflated "breeches" grows on the top part of the stalk. Each flower is about ³/₄ inch (18 mm) long. The plants are low growing with deeply lobed leaves. Rocky slopes, along streams, open woods. Ozark Region, Polk County. March-May.

MUSTARD FAMILY (Cruciferae)

B YELLOW ROCKET   *Barbarea vulgaris*

The bright yellow flowers have 6 stamens. The seed pods are about 1 inch (2.5 cm) in length. The lower leaves usually have 5 lobes with the terminal one larger and smooth edged. Upper leaves are sessile, not lobed but toothed. Native of Europe. Near streams, fields, meadows. Scattered over the state. April-July.

B. verna, Winter Cress, has 5- 10 pairs of lobes on the lower leaves, and pods up to 3 inches (7.5 cm) long. Also a native of Europe. Central counties. *Arabis canadensis,* Sickle Pod, is a tall species with small cream-colored flowers at the top part of the plant and up to 4 inch (10 cm) long pods which point downward. Occurs over the northern half of the state and blooms during March-June. *A. laevigaia* is similar with white blooms. Slopes, rocky areas, hillsides.

Brassica is the genus which includes Leaf Mustard, Turnip and Charlock. All 3 species are cultivated, introduced species with yellow flowers and are somewhat like species of *Barbarea*.

C SPRING CRESS   **Cardamine bulbosa*

The white flowers are about ¹/₃ inch (8mm) wide with 4 petals in the form of a cross. Oval basal leaves, stem leaves usually toothed. *Cardamine* species can be recognized by their early blooming period. This species has bulblike roots. Wet, open areas, open woods, roadsides. There are 8 species in this genus in Arkansas. Some are well distributed over the state. March- June.

Capsella bursa-pastoris, Shepherd's Purse, is the only species of the genus in Arkansas and is a weedy plant with very small whitish flowers. It is best recognized by the triangular or "purse-shaped" seed pods on long pedicels. Occurs statewide; also a world-wide species. Blooms throughout the year.

D TOOTHWORT   **Dentaria laciniata*

White, pinkish or lavender blooms are about ¹/₂ inch (13 mm) wide and somewhat tubular at the base. Flowering usually begins before the basal leaves appear. Long, toothed leaves that vary in width are in whorls of 3 with up to 3 lobes each. Slopes in woodlands, near streams. Well distributed in the Ozark and Ouachita Mountain regions, also Crowley's Ridge. February-May.

A

B

C

D

A WESTERN WALL-FLOWER   *Erysimum capitatum*

A large flowered mustard with orange flowers and long slender pods. Flowers are nearly ³/₄ inch (18 mm) across. Slender, slightly toothed leaves. Rocky soils. Logan, Faulkner and Sharp counties are the only reported locations at this time. May-July. Biennial.

B DAME'S ROCKET   *Hesperis matronalis*

A variable species with pink or sometimes white or purplish blooms up to 2 inches (5 cm) wide. The plants are up to 3 feet (1 meter) tall with toothed or rounded leaves. A cultivated flower from England and other European and Asian countries that has escaped in local areas and may become more widespread. Roadsides, old house sites, gardens, etc. Reported from a few northern counties and Pulaski County. May-August.

C WATER CRESS   **Nasturtium officinale*

The very small, 4-petaled white flowers are in groups at the tips of the stems. A creeping plant with rounded leaves. The stems float on the water. The thick, fleshy vegetation has been used in salads. The vegetation is eaten by deer, aquatic animals and waterfowl. Springs, clear streams. Mainly in Ozark Region counties, some Ouachita Mountain Region counties. April -September.

D SELENIA   *Selenia aurea*

Bright yellow flowers. The plants are short, well under 1 foot (25 cm) high, with leaves divided into very narrow, fernlike segments. Thick stands often occur. Rocky glades, table rock, rocky slopes and roadbanks. Scattered in the Ozark and Ouachita Mountain regions. March-May.

A

B

C

D

A STREPTANTHUS   *Streptanthus squamiformis*

The reddish to reddish-purple flowers have dark centers from which dark veins extend into the petals. The buds are pale pink to whitish. The flowers are in spikes and the upper stems, sepals and pedicels have fine hairs (pubescent). Oval-shaped leaves clasp the stems. The plants grow to 3 feet (1 meter) high or higher. Rocky hillsides, roadsides. Recorded in Howard and Polk counties. May-June.

 * *S. maculatus*, Twist-flower, has similar flowers in racernes and has been found in a limited number of central counties. *S. hyacinthoides* has plants like the above with somewhat tubular purple and white flowers in a raceme up to 1 foot (30 cm) long. Buds are erect to horizontal and the flowers are drooping. Reported from Nevada and Ouachita counties on sandy soils. May- June.

CAPER FAMILY (Capparaceae)

B SPIDER FLOWER   **Cleome spinosa*

A large "spidery" white to pinkish flower that has escaped cultivation. The leaves have prickles and 5-7 leaflets. Plants are 3 feet (1 meter) or more in height. Native of South America. Roadsides, railroads, old garden sites. Reported from scattered counties over the northern two- thirds of the state but may have escaped in other locations. May-September. Annual.

C CLAMMY-WEED   *Polanisia dodecandra*

Small, white flowers about $1/2$ inch (13 mm) wide are in the tops of the plants. The seed pods angle upward from the stalks. The plants are clammy or sticky with leaves divided into 3 pointed segments. Along streams, gravel bars, moist ground. Northern counties, a few Ouachita Mountain Region counties. May-September.

STONECROP FAMILY (Crassulaceae)

The genus *Sedum*, in Arkansas, includes 5 species. Two of these are cultivated species that sometimes escape cultivation.

D YELLOW SEDUM   *Sedum nuttallianum*

The small yellow flowers have sharp-pointed petals and are in clusters along the branches. The plants are only a few inches (cm) high with fleshy stems and leaves. Grows in clumps. Rocky glades, table rock, bluffs, and ledges. Found mainly in a few Ozark Region counties and Montgomery and Pike counties in the Ouachita Mountain Region. April-June.

 S. ternatum, a white flowered species, has been found in a few, widely scattered counties.

94

A

B

C

D

A   WIDOW'S CROSS   *Sedum pulchellum*

Similar to Yellow Sedum but a larger plant with more numerous pink flowers. More widely distributed in both the Ozark and Ouachita Mountain regions.

SUNDEW FAMILY (Droseraceae)

Sundew is the only species of this family that occurs in the state.

B   SUNDEW   *Drosera brevifolia*

The pink or occasionally white flowers are less than $\frac{1}{2}$ inch (13 mm) wide. Reddish leaves in a basal rosette are equipped with sticky, leaf hairs which trap insects, rolling over them and later digesting them. Insect skeletons can usually be found in the rolled leaves. The plants are only a few inches (cm) tall. Sandy or boggy sites. Mainly in southern counties but extending to a few northcentral counties, Benton County. April-June.

SAXIFRAGE FAMILY (Saxifragaceae)

C   ROCK GERANIUM, ALUMROOT   *Heuchera americana*

The small yellowish, drooping flowers are about $\frac{1}{4}$ inch (6 mm) long on a tall slender flower stalk. The stamens with orange anthers protrude from the flowers. The leaves are attractive with long stalked, rounded blades. Rocky bluffs and ledges, rocky soils. Mainly in Ozark Region counties and a few Ouachita Mountain Region counties. April-June.

D   ARKANSAS ALUMROOT (ENDEMIC)   *Heuchera villosa var. arkansana*

The small white flowers are in dense clusters on short stalks. The leaves are large and attractive, somewhat hairy. Two varieties have been listed: *villosa* and *arkansana*. Shady ledges and bluffs, especially where there is a good moisture supply. Occasionally along streams. A few Ozark Region counties. Late August-October.

A

B

C

D

A   WILD HYDRANGEA   *Hydrangea arborescens*

There are flat or dome-shaped clusters of small white flowers. A few large sterile flowers occur around the edges of the clusters which often measure several inches (cm) across. This plant is a shrub up to 5 feet (1.5 meters) tall. Cultivated forms have been developed that produce a large number of the sterile flowers. Furnishes food for deer. Turkeys feed upon the flowers and fruits. Damp woods, slopes, bluffs, along streams. Its presence indicates a good moisture supply. Better drained upland soils over the state. May-July.

B   MITERWORT   *Mitella diphylla*

Small, whitish flowers are in a slender spike above the leaves. Upon close examination the flowers resemble a small snowflake because of the many slender, angled lobes of the petals. There is a pair of opposite leaves on the stalk. The plants may grow singly or in clumps. Along rocky streams, moist rocky areas, mossy banks. Reported from Stone County only at this time. April-June.

C   GRASS-OF-PARNASSUS   *Parnassia grandifolia*

The white flowers are about 1 inch (2.5 cm) wide with green veins in the petals. A single, rounded leaf clasps the stalk about midway. Other leaves are basal. The plants are about 1-1½ feet (30-45 cm) tall. Along streams, rocky wet soils, especially on limestone. Reported from several counties in the northcentral part of the Ozark Region, also Polk County. August- October.

D   DITCH STONECROP   *Penthorum sedoides*

Small, yellowish-green flowers with reddish-brown stamens grow along one side of the flower stalk. Flowers are similar to those of the genus *Sedum* in the Stonecrop Family. Plants are up to 2 feet (60 cm) high with sharply toothed, lanceolate to oblong leaves. Wet soils. Statewide. July-October.

A

B

C

D

A   PALMER'S SAXIFRAGE   *Saxifraga palmeri*

Small, white flowers about ¼ inch (6 mm) wide are at the tops of the stalks and begin to bloom while the plants are still small. The stalks and leaves are hairy. Plants may reach 1 foot (30 cm) in height. Leaves are mainly basal. Streamsides, open or wooded rocky areas. Well distributed in the Ozark Region, less frequent in the Ouachita Mountain Region. March-May.

ROSE FAMILY (Rosaceae)

B   GOAT'S BEARD   *Aruncus dioicus*

The white to yellowish- white, tiny flowers are in long branching plumes. Flowers are single- sexed, with the male and female flowers on separate plants. A tall shrub up to 5 feet (1.5 meters) or more in height. Compound, toothed leaves. Damp, wooded areas, slopes. Shade tolerant. Mainly in Ozark Region counties and on Crowley's Ridge. May-July.

C   INDIAN STRAWBERRY   *Duchesnea indica*

The yellow flowers are ¾ inch (18 mm) wide with narrow or rounded petals. The fruit resembles a small strawberry but has little taste. The plants are creeping with 3-parted leaves that are toothed. Native of Asia. Open woods, idle or disturbed land, shady areas, often near buildings. Statewide. March-June.

D   WILD STRAWBERRY   **Fragaria virginianum*

Similar to Indian Strawberry but has white flowers and is more northern in distribution. Birds and animals eat the fruit of both species, also browsed by deer. A native plant with true strawberry flavor. April-May.

A

B

C

D

A WHITE AVENS   *Geum canadense*

The white flowers are on spreading, slender stalks in the top part of the plant. Flowers are solitary at the ends of the branches. The fruit is a burlike group of seeds. The leaves are 3 lobed, toothed and pointed. The plants grow to about 2 feet (60 cm) high. Occasionally browsed by deer. Turkeys eat the seeds in fall and winter. Moist woodland soils, often near bodies of water. Shade tolerant. Statewide. May-August.

B AMERICAN IPECAC   ** Gillenia stipulatus*

White, irregularly shaped narrow petals spread out stiffly giving the flower a starlike appearance. Flowers are up to 1 inch (2.5 cm) wide. The 3-parted leaves have small stipules. The plants grow to about 3 feet (1 meter) tall. The generic name was formerly *Porteranthus.* Woodlands. May become abundant in burned or disturbed areas. Statewide. May-July.

C ROUGH-FRUITED CINQUEFOIL   *Potentilla recta*

The symmetrical yellow flowers have notched petals and yellow stamens. Flowers are $^3/_4$ inch (18 mm) wide. Upright, sturdy plants with uniformly shaped, toothed leaves. Grows to about 2 feet (60 cm) high. Often in large colonies. Native of Europe. Roadsides, idle land. Nearly statewide but not common in the Delta or Gulf Coastal Plain regions. May-August.

D CINQUEFOIL, FIVE-FINGER   *Potentilla simplex*

The yellow flowers are $^1/_2$ inch (13 mm) wide with rounded petals. Palmately compound leaves with 5 leaflets. A low growing vine. Cinquefoil is French for "5-leaves." A preferred deer food plant during the growing season. Often on thin, dry soils, roadsides, fields, openings in woods. Statewide. May-July.

A

B

C

D

Nine species in the genus *Rosa* have been discovered in Arkansas.

A MULTIFLORA ROSE   *Rosa multiflora*

Clusters of small white or, rarely, pink flowers are on large plants often growing 8 feet (2.4 meters) high and 12 feet (3.6 meters) across with long, arching branches. Has been used for fences and wildlife cover. Readily escapes to fencerows and woods. The fruits or hips are eaten by birds. Native of Asia. May-June.

B PRAIRIE ROSE, CLIMBING ROSE   *Rosa setigera*

White or reddish flowers. In this species the leaflets are in groups of 3 on old stems and often in groups of 5 on young stems. The thorns are curved or hooked on the thick, climbing stems. Browsed by deer. Old fields, roadsides, fencerows, open woods, thickets. Over most of the state except for some Delta Region and Gulf Coastal Plain Region counties. May-July.

   R. carolina, Pasture Rose, has straight thorns, leaflets in groups of 3 to 7 and occurs statewide. The plants are short with slender, wiry stems.

C MEMORIAL ROSE   *Rosa wichuraiana*

A white rose with bright yellow stamens. Sometimes pink flowers occur. Smooth stems bear semi-evergreen leaves with 7-9 leaflets. The thorns are broad at the base, curved and flat. This is an escaped rose that was derived from Multiflora Rose. Road banks, idle land, old home sites. Southern counties. May-June.

Rubus contains at least 13 species in Arkansas. Identification to species is very difficult.

D DEWBERRY   *Rubus flagellaris*

The crisp white flowers grow along the main stems. The fruit is similar to the blackberry but larger. Flowers are about $^3/_4$ inch (18 mm) wide. The vines are thorny with leaves in groups of 5. Raspberries and blackberries belong to this genus. Dewberries are creeping whereas the blackberry and raspberries are more erect. Both dewberry and blackberry plants are browsed by deer. The berries and seeds are used for food by several wildlife species. A variety of soils and sites. Statewide. April-June.

A

B

C

D

A   HARDHACK, STEEPLE BUSH   *Spiraea tomentosa*

Very small pink flowers occur in pointed clusters at the tops of the plants. An upright shrub with oblong, toothed leaves that are hairy on the underside. Brownish stems. Open woods, sandy soils. Four central counties, Greene County. Arkansas is apparently on the southwestern border of the range of this species. July- September.

PEA, BEAN OR LEGUME FAMILY (Leguminosae)

The Legume Family includes many species that furnish food for wildlife.

B   GROUNDNUT   *Apios americana*

Maroon to dull red and white flowers are in tight groups or racemes that grow out of the leaf axils. Each flower is about $^1/_2$ inch (13 mm) long. The leaves are pinnately compound with 5-7 leaflets. A vine species that often climbs upon other vegetation. Indians and early settlers ate the tubers. Low ground, open areas or thickets. Statewide. July-September.

C   RATTLE WEED   *Astragalus canadensis*

There are up to 70 cream or light yellow flowers in an inflorescence up to 4 inches (10 cm) long. Each flower is about 1 inch (2.5 cm) long. The plumlike fruits do not open or open late in the season. Pinnately compound leaves on plants up to 5 feet (1.5 meters) tall. Rocky or well drained soils. Mainly in the Ozark Region. April-July.

D   GROUND PLUM   *Astragalus crassicarpus var. trichocalyx*

The cream or yellowish tubular flowers are in tight groups just above the leaves. Each flower is about 1 inch (2.5 cm) long. The plants are about 1 foot (30 cm) tall when in bloom. There are many closely grouped leaflets on the pinnately compound leaves. Rocky slopes, open woods, glades. Northwestern counties, a few Ouachita Mountain Region counties, also Ouachita County. March-May.

There are 6 other species and varieties of *Astragalus* - mainly in western and southwestern counties. *A. distortus*, Bent Milk Vetch, is a low, creeping plant with small leaves and purplish to lilac flowers. Found in open areas on limestone or shale.

A

B

C

D

A   BLUE FALSE INDIGO   *Baptisia australis*

The purple flowers are in racemes at the ends of the upright stalks. The plants are up to 4 feet (1.2 meters) high with trifoliate leaves that have rounded leaflets. The sap is purple. This plant can be grown from seed. Limestone glades and prairies. Extreme northern Ozark Region counties, also Crawford and Sebastian counties. May-June.

B   WHITE WILD INDIGO   ** Baptisia leucantha*

White, pealike flowers grow on long, upright stalks. Blooming begins at the bottom of the inflorescense. The plant branches outward with trifoliate leaves and may reach 5 feet (1.5 meters) in height. Roadsides and banks, levees, prairies, glades. Statewide. May throughout the summer.

C   LONG-BRACTED WILD INDIGO   *Baptisia leucophaea*

The cream-colored flowers are in a long, tapering inflorescense that points downward and is borne in the lower part of the plant. The low, bushy plants fade to a lead-gray color with the leaves persisting for long periods. Often on thin, bare soils along roadways, slopes, etc. Nearly statewide. April-June.

B. nuttalliana, Nuttall Indigo, is vegetatively similar to other species in the genus but the small yellow flowers are scattered over the entire plant. This species is mainly limited to the Gulf Coastal Plain Region.

D   YELLOW WILD INDIGO   *Baptisia sphaerocarpa*

The yellow flowers are in upright racemes in the tops of the plants. The bushy, rounded plants have trifoliate leaves. Pinelands, sandy soils, roadsides. Central and western counties. April- June.

A

B

C

D

A   PARTRIDGE PEA   ** Cassia fasciculata*

Numerous, bright yellow, showy flowers with brownish centers are up to 1^1/$_2$ inches (3.8 cm) wide with wide petals. Compound leaves with small leaflets on plants up to about 3 feet (1 meter) high. An annual that has been used in wildlife plantings for quail, turkey and other gamebirds. Variety of soils, open areas. Statewide. Summer into fall.

B   WILD SENNA   ** Cassia marilandica*

The bright yellow flowers have brownish centers and narrow petals that are often curled and are smaller than those of Partridge Pea. The compound leaves are larger than those of Partridge Pea. A perennial, with plants up to 6 feet (1.8 meters) tall. Roadsides, railroads, open woods, levees. Nearly statewide but not common in the Delta and Gulf Coastal Plain regions. July-August.

   * C. obtusifolia, Sickepod, and *C. occidentalis*, Coffee Senna, are two tall weedy plants that invade cultivated fields. Also found in ditches, low open areas. Both are natives of tropical countries. They have curved pods, pealike yellow flowers and pinnately compound leaves with rounded segments. *Sesbania macrocarpa*, Coffee Bean, is a very tall, smooth plant with spreading branches. The flowers are yellow, pealike and scattered over the stems in loose groups of a few flowers each. The leaves are pinnately compound with many short, narrow segments. The long, very slender pods hold many hard seeds which are eaten by quail. These plants are common to rice fields, cultivated areas, ditches or other low ground. More common in southern and eastern counties. May-October.

C   BUTTERFLY PEA   *Centrosema virginianum*

Violet colored flowers 1^1/$_2$ inches (3.8 cm) wide have a white central marking. The keel is without wings and is upward. The leaflets of the trifoliate leaves are pointed and vary in shape from oval to lanceolate. An important quail food plant. Dry areas, cutover timberlands, sandy soils. Common in Gulf Coastal Plain Region counties, scattered elsewhere. June-August.

D   BUTTERFLY PEA   *Clitoria mariana*

Somewhat similar to *Centrosema virginianum* but with a winged keel that is downward. The standard petal is boat-shaped. The large flowers are over 2 inches (5 cm) long. Well drained soils. Nearly statewide. June- August.

A

B

C

D

A CROWN VETCH   *Coronilla varia*

The small pink and white flowers are in tight round clusters or "crowns" Small, compound, vetchlike leaves. A perennial plant that is native to Europe, Asia, Africa. Has been planted for ground cover along highways, etc. and often escapes. Variety of soils, fields, lots, edges of woods, roadsides. Mainly in Ozark Region counties. May bloom throughout the summer.

B PRAIRIE MIMOSA, ILLINOIS MIMOSA   *Desmanthus illinoensis*

Tiny flowers in ball-shaped clusters at the tops of the plants are white in color. The leaves are double pinnately compound. The fruits are curved into round structures. Roadsides, open areas, prairies. Statewide. June-August.

  Acacia angustissima, Prairie Acacia, is similar but has more slender and shorter filaments in the flower head than the above species. This species has oblong seed pods. The seeds are used as food by wildlife. Both species furnish deer browse. Found mainly in northern counties.

  Desmodium is the genus including beggar's lice and tick trefoil species; 16 species are listed for the state. There are both pink and white flowered species. Both the seeds and leaves are important wildlife foods.

C TICK TREFOIL, BEGGAR'S LICE   *Desmodium spp.*

Purplish, pink, reddish or occasionally white, pealike flowers occur in clusters or small groups at or near the ends of the stems. The calyx has an upper and lower lip. Trifoliate leaves on plants that are mainly upright, but low growing or creeping forms also occur. The triangular or oval seed pods that adhere to clothing are familiar to most people. The seeds are eaten by quail and turkeys and the plants are browsed by deer. Roadsides, woodlands, disturbed soils. Statewide. Summer into fall.

D CORAL BEAN   *Erythrina herbacea*

The deep red, tubular flowers are in spikes on long stalks. The flowers are about 2 inches (5 cm) long. The pods split open exposing scarlet berries which cling to the pods. The leaves are trifoliate with the leaflets having pointed tips. A perennial plant 2-4 feet (60-120 cm) tall. Sandy soils. Collected in Columbia and Union counties. April-June.

A

B

C

D

A   BLADDER POD   *Glottidium vesicarium*

Individual flowers are ¹/₂ inch (13mm) or less in length with yellow petals edged with red. They are in short racemes on slender stems. The seed pods are short and wide and contain 2 seeds. The plants are tall, 7 feet (2.1 meters) or so, with spreading branches and pinnately compound leaves. Similar to *Sesbania* species. Dry sandy soils or moist soils. Mainly in southern and central counties. July-September.

B   SINGLETARY PEA   *Lathyrus hirsutus*

The flowers are about ¹/₂ inch (13 mm) long, one or two to each cluster, and vary in color from pale lavender to reddish-purple. The leaves and stems are flattened and resemble the vegetation of the sweetpea which was derived from this genus. The leaves have two slender segments. Alien. Dry areas, roadsides, idle land. Nearly statewide, common in the Delta Region counties. April-July.

C   EVERLASTING PEA   *Lathyrus latifolius*

The white to pink or deep shades of rose to rose-purple flowers are in racernes on straight leafless stalks. Not fragrant. The plants are creeping or will climb by means of tendrils. The stems are keeled or winged. The plant has heavy foliage and may cover sizeable areas. Alien. Fencerows, roadsides, old homesites, lots. Statewide in scattered locations. May and throughout the summer.

Lespedeza is a genus of bush-clovers, including many species and hybrids. Some are cultivated. There is only one seed in each seed pod. The flowers are small and pink to red, yellow or white. The leaves and seeds of most of the species are important wildlife foods.

D   HAIRY BUSH CLOVER   *Lespedeza hirta*

The flowers are creamy-white to yellowish and in clusters on stalks that project beyond the leaves. The plants are covered with light-colored hairs. The leaflets are rounded. Dry sites in woodland openings, old fields. Statewide, less frequent in Delta Region counties, Crowley's Ridge. August-October.

A

B

C

D

A   SLENDER BUSH COVER   *Lespedeza virginica*

The reddish or reddish-purple flowers are crowded in the leaf axils in the top part of the plants. The leaves have narrow segments about 1-2 inches (2.5-5 cm) long. The upright, slightly branching plants are 2-4 feet (60-120 cm) tall. A variety of soils and sites, fields, roadsides, open woods, cutover land. Statewide. May- September.

L. bicolor is a tall, woody perennial with spreading branches and numerous small pink flowers over the entire top part of the plant. Produces seeds which are highly sought after by quail and other birds and is therefore used in plantings for wildlife. This species has escaped in several central counties. Native of Japan. August-October.

The genus *Medicago* includes cultivated species such as the bur-clovers and alfalfa. The wild species of this genus are similar to other clovers which are illustrated or described.

Melilotus is the genus including the tall white and yellow sweet clovers which are cultivated species. These have become naturalized.

B   YELLOW-PUFF   *Neptunia lutea*

Yellow, ball-shaped flower heads with many protruding stamens create a spherical, fluffy appearing flower cluster about 1 inch (2.5 cm) in diameter. Small, pinnately compound leaves on creeping stems. These plants are not armed with spines. Roadsides, railroads, prairies, pinelands. Gulf Coastal Plain Region counties and in the Arkansas River Valley counties. June-September.

C   WHITE PRAIRIE CLOVER   *Petalostemon candidum*

Tassellike flower heads about 1¹/₂ inches(3.8cm) in length have small white flowers in a ring around the cone-shaped base. Blooming progresses from the bottom of the head upward. Slender trifoliate leaves on plants 2-2¹/₂feet (60-75 cm) tall. Prairies, open woods and glades, rocky slopes, ledges. Reported from over most of the state except for the southeastern quarter. May-August.

D   PURPLE PRAIRIE CLOVER   **Petalostemon purpureum*

Similar to White Prairie Clover but with rose colored flowers. Collected from a few southwestern counties and from northern counties of the Ozark Region. Prefers limestone soils. May-August.

A

B

C

D

A SAMPSON'S SNAKEROOT *Psoralea psoralioides*

Light bluish to purplish flowers occur in terminal clusters. Long, leafless flower stalks. A bushy, perennial plant with trifoliate leaves 2-3 inches (5-7.5 cm) long. The plants are about 2 feet (60 cm) tall. Pinelands, roadsides, railroads, prairies. Statewide. April-June.

P. simplex, an upright, purple-flowered species, occurs in central counties.

B SNOUTBEAN *Rhynchosia latifolia*

The bright yellow flowers produce flat pods. The flowers are about $\frac{1}{2}$ inch (13 mm) long. The plants are trailing to semi-erect and hairy. Pinelands, sandy open areas. Widespread except for the Delta Region. June-August.

Crotolaria spp., Rattlebox, has yellow pealike flowers on low plants that produce inflated, football-shaped pods that turn dark with age. Upon aging the dry seeds rattle inside the pods. Statewide. May-September.

C SENSITIVE BRIER *Schrankia nuttallii*

Pink to pinkish-purple, spherical flower heads with the individual small flowers having several yellow-tipped stamens protruding. The fruit is a flat prickly pod. Narrow, doubly compound leaves have many pairs of small leaflets that fold together when disturbed. There are many prickles or spines on these plants. A perennial that trails along the ground. The leaves are eaten by turkeys and other wildlife. Usually on thin soil in open areas. Statewide. May- September.

Mimosa strigillosa, Powderpuff , is similar but is without spines. Southern counties. April- August.

D PENCIL FLOWER *Stylosanthes biflora*

The yellow to nearly orange flowers often are in pairs. The upper petal or standard is rounded. The flowers are about $\frac{3}{8}$ inch (1 cm) wide. The trifoliate leaves are on short stems. A low growing plant with upright stems bearing the flowers. The seeds are utilized for food by quail and turkeys. Open woods, trails, roadsides, slopes, cutovers. Statewide. May-September.

Strophostyles umbellata, Wild Bean, is a low-growing, slender vine with round pink flower groups on slender bare stalks 3-4 inches (7.5-10 cm) long. Occurs nearly statewide and blooms during July-September. A perennial. The seeds are eaten by bobwhite quail and wild turkey.

A

B

C

D

A   GOAT'S RUE   *Tephrosia virginiana*

Yellow, or white and pink flowers about ¾ inch (18 mm) wide are arranged in whorls at the tops of the plants. The leaves are compound and vetchlike on the hairy plants. The upright branches grow to about 2 feet (60 cm) high. The roots contain rotenone. The seeds are eaten by various game birds. Dry soils, open areas. Statewide. April-June.

B   HOARY PEA, DEVIL'S SHOE LACES   *Tephrosia onobrychoides*

The white flowers turn a deep red color upon aging. The flower stalks are long with few leaves in the upper part and are usually straight. A slightly down-curved, flat pod is produced that is about 2-3 inches (5-7.5 cm) long at maturity. The leaf segments are oblong on reddish stems. The plants are hairy. Sandy or rocky soils along roads or in old fields and other idle ground. Mainly in southern and central counties. May-August.

The genus *Trifolium* contains the clovers. Some are cultivated and some are native wild species. The flowers are in heads or spikes. The upper petal or standard is folded over. A few of the more showy and common species are treated. Some species are valuable for wildlife plantings. Both the seeds and the foliage are used as food by wildlife.

C   CRIMSON CLOVER   *Trifolium incarnatum*

Easily identified by the crimson or scarlet flower heads. Used as a soil builder or soil stabilizing ground cover planting. A native of Eurasia. Roadways, open areas, fields. Statewide. April-June. Annual.

T. arvense, Rabbit-foot Clover, can be recognized by the long, grayish heads which have a fuzzy appearance suggesting a rabbit's foot. A cultivated species. Occurs over most of the state. May-August.

D   RED CLOVER   *Trifolium pratense*

Reddish to reddish-purple flower heads. Typical trifoliate leaves with a light green "v" shaped design on each lobe. A hairy plant that is cultivated and has escaped throughout the state. Fields, open areas, pastures, meadows, roadsides. Statewide. April-August.

A

B

C

D

A WHITE CLOVER   *Trifolium repens*

White to light pink flowers. The rounded flower head is ¹/₂-³/₄ inch (13-18 mm) in diameter. Leaves trifoliate with light green "v" markings. Usually a low growing plant in lawns but in other areas may grow to 1 foot (30 cm) high. A cultivated species. Lawns, pastures, fields. Statewide. Spring and summer months but also occasionally in other months.

   T. resupinatum, Persian Clover, is a slender, annual species with small rose-purple heads. It occurs in lawns, along streets and roadsides. It is an introduced species that is found mainly in the southern part of the state, especially near cities and towns. March-June.

B WOOD VETCH   *Vicia caroliniana*

White, slender flowers, occasionally with pink tints. Open, pinnately compound leaves. A climbing or trailing plant. A native vetch. Woodlands, openings, roadsides, cutover land. Common over most of the state except for the Delta Region. April-June.

C SMOOTH VETCH   * *Vicia dasycarpa*

The flowers are reddish-purple with white tips. Each flower is about ¹/₂ inch (13 mm) long and short stalked. This plant is an annual that climbs by means of slender tendrils. There are 5-10 pairs of leaflets. The plants are glabrous or have very short hairs. Native of Europe that is planted and has escaped in many areas. Quail feed upon the seeds of several species of vetch. Variety of open sites. Statewide. April -September.

   V. grandiflora, Bigflower Vetch, has large yellow flowers without central brown markings. Planted along roadsides in central Arkansas.

D COMMON VETCH   *Vicia sativa*

The rounded, reddish-purple flowers are sometimes nearly 1 inch (2.5 cm) long and often in pairs. The pinnately compound leaves have 8-16 segments that are linear to oblong in shape. Tendrils extend from the ends of the leaves. Alien from Europe. Fields, open idle land. Statewide, less common in mountainous areas. March-August.

   Wisteria, spp., Wild Wisteria. Two wild vine species occur in the state and can usually be distinguished from cultivated species by their smaller, more compact inflorescences. April- June.

A

B

C

D

FLAX FAMILY (Linaceae)

Four species, all in the genus *Linum*, represent the family in Arkansas.

A   FLAX   *Linum medium*

The pale yellow flowers are less than $1/2$ inch (13 mm) wide on slender stalks. The petals are thin and delicate and are closed during the middle part of the day. The leaves in the upper part of the plant grow close to the branches which angle upward. The plants are usually less than 2 feet (60 cm) high. Poor, thin soils, open areas. Statewide. June-August.

WOOD SORREL FAMILY (Oxalidaceae)

B   CREEPING LADY'S SORREL   *Oxalis corniculata*

Small plants with yellow flowers and light green, cloverlike leaves. Somewhat hairy with a creeping stem. Large brown stipules. Alien. Adapted to various soils and sites. Statewide. April-frost.

0. stricta, Yellow Wood Sorrel, is somewhat like the above with larger flowers and leaves and erect seedpods. An upright plant that is more common in northern Arkansas. The seeds furnish food for quail and turkeys.

C   VIOLET WOOD SORREL   *Oxalis violacea*

Lavender, violet or nearly white flowers usually have dark streaks on the petals. The flowers are about $3/4$ inch (18 mm) wide with the 5 petals joined at the base. The cloverlike leaves are notched or heart-shaped and often have brownish streaks. Plants are 6-8 inches (15-20 cm) tall. A variety of sites and soils. Statewide. April-June.

0. rubra, Rose Wood Sorrel, is a red, cultivated species that has spread to fields and roadsides. It has been reported from a few central and southern counties. March-September.

GERANIUM FAMILY (Geraniaceae)

D   PINK NEEDLE   *Erodium cicutarium*

The rose colored flowers are less than $1/2$ inch (13 mm) wide. Feathery, twice-pinnately compound leaves appear fernlike, often lying close to the ground. Alien. Lots, lawns, roadsides. Scattered counties in the western half of the state. April-October.

A

B

C

D

A   CAROLINA CRANESBILL   *Geranium carolinianum*

The pale lavender to nearly white flowers are slightly over $^1/_4$ inch (6 mm) wide. Plants are usually not over 1 foot (30 cm) high. Weedy. The seeds furnish food for quail, turkeys and doves. Fields, gardens, vacant lots, idle land. Common over the entire state. March-July.

B   WILD GERANIUM , SPOTTED CRANESBILL   *Geranium maculatum*

The flowers are pink to reddish-purple with dark veins in the petals and are about 1 inch (2.5 cm) wide. The long slender fruits suggest the bill of a waterbird. Opposite leaves with 5 pointed lobes often are spotted with rusty or light colored markings. Upper leaves may have only 3 lobes. A perennial that grows to about 2 feet (60 cm) tall. Open or shaded woodlands, benches, roadbanks, streamsides. Over much of the state except for the Delta Region. More common in the Ozark and Ouachita Mountain regions. April-May.

MILKWORT FAMILY (Polygalaceae)

All 9 species of the family in this state are in the genus *Polygala*.

C   CROSS-LEAVED POLYGALA, CANDYROOT   *Polygala cruciata*

These unusual flower spikes somewhat resemble small paper lanterns. They are pink or white with pink edges and are about 2 inches (5 cm) in length. The plants grow to about 1 foot (30 cm) high with slender leaves in the form of a cross. Wet or dry sandy soils, often in pinelands. Has been recorded in 6 counties: Ashley, Benton, Calhoun, Faulkner, Grant and Saline. April- June.

D   BACHELOR'S BUTTON   *Polygala nana*

The yellow flower heads are somewhat thimble-shaped with a fringed appearance and are about $1^1/_2$ inches (3.8 cm) long. The leaves are basal and linear to spatulate. The plants are short, usually less than 6 inches (15 cm) high. Sandy soil in pinelands. Recorded in Ashley, Bradley and Calhoun counties. Arkansas is apparently at the northwestern extremity of the range of the species. April-June.

A

B

C

D

A   MILKWORT   *Polygala sanguinea*

White to pink flowers are tightly packed into the small heads which are usually less than 1 inch (2.5 cm) long. The plants are slender with only a few alternate leaves. Fields, meadows, open areas. Statewide. June-September.

B   SENECA SNAKEROOT   *Polygala senega*

The white rounded flowers are in pointed racemes 2-3 inches (5-7.5 cm) long. Alternate.leaves. The stems are usually not branched. Plants are up to 1$\frac{1}{2}$ feet (45 cm) high. Slopes, wooded valleys, often on limestone soils. Ozark Region, also Grant County. May-July.

C   WHORLED MILKWORT   *Polygala verticillata*

Very similar in appearance to Seneca Snakeroot except that the plants and racemes of flowers are more slender. The leaves are in whorls of 3-6. Often on thin dry soils, roadsides, open woods. Statewide. May-September.

SPURGE FAMILY (Euphorbiaceae)

D   BULL NETTLE   *Cnidoscolus texanus*

The white flowers are over 1 inch (2.5 cm) wide. The fruit is a 3-celled spiney capsule. Branching stems and crinkled leaves are all armed with stiff hairs and stinging spines. Plants grow to 3 feet (1 meter) tall. The seeds are sometimes eaten by quail. Sandy, pineland soils. A few southwestern counties of the Gulf Coastal Plain Region, Pope County. April-July.

A

B

C

D

A   SNOW-ON-THE-PRAIRIE   *Euphorbia bicolor*

Inconspicuous, small white flowers with pale yellow centers are located mainly in the top part of the plants. The leaves are the noticeable feature of this plant. They are long and slender, pale green and edged with a white margin giving the plant a ghostlike appearance from a distance. Sandy open areas, pastures. Southwestern Gulf Coastal Plain Region counties, Polk County. September-November.

B   WOOD SPURGE   *Euphorbia commutata*

The greenish-yellow, small flowers are in rounded clusters that hang in pairs inside the round, cupped floral leaves. The plants are a foot (30 cm) or more in height with oval, alternate leaves. Along streams, woodland edges, wooded slopes. Mainly in Ozark Region counties and a few Ouachita Mountain Region counties. April-June.

C   FLOWERING SPURGE   *Euphorbia corollata*

The bright, chalky-white flowers are single sexed. What appear to be petals are actually 5 lobes. The flowers are in flat groups across the tops of the plants and are only $1/4$ inch (6 mm) wide. The male flowers have only one stamen. The oblong leaves alternate up the stalks and form a whorl of 3-4 where the stems branch. The sap is sticky and white. Deer feed upon the plants in spring and summer. Adapted to many types of sites. Statewide. May-October.

D   WILD POINSETTIA   *Euphorbia cyathophora*

The flower parts are without lobes and have only a single small gland. Red patches of variable shape and size occur at the base of the leaflike bracts. The bracts and leaves vary in shape. More commonly known as *E. heterophylla,* as used by most authors. Valleys, streamsides, open or wooded sites. Most common in the Ozark Region. Also in a few Ouachita Mountain Region and southern counties. August-October.

A

B

C

D

TOUCH-M&NOT or BALSAM FAMILY

A   JEWEL-WEED, SPOTTED TOUCH-ME-NOT   *Impatiens capensis*

The reddish-orange flowers have brown spots on the front of the petals and a curled sac or tail. The fruit is a capsule that flips open when disturbed, throwing out the seeds. Flowers are about 1 inch (2.5 cm) long. The leaves are oval with pointed ends and smooth-surfaced with toothed edges. Large colonies sometimes occur. The plants are 5-6 feet (1.5-1.8 meters) tall on favorable sites. Deer use the plants for food. Moist sites, both open and shaded. Statewide. May-October.

B   PALE TOUCH-ME-NOT   *Impatiens pallida*

Similar to the above with yellow flowers. Occurs mainly in the Ozark Region, also in Pulaski and Lonoke counties. The seeds are occasionally eaten by quail.

BUCKTHORN FAMILY (Rhamnaceae)

C   NEW JERSEY TEA   *Ceanothus americanus*

Very small white flowers are in rounded upright clusters. Plants begin to bloom while still small in size. A rounded shrub up to nearly 3 feet (1 meter) tall when mature. The leaves are hairy on the underside and are occasionally eaten by deer. The fruits are eaten by wild turkeys and quail. Woodland edges, roadsides, prairies, often on dry soils. May-June.

MALLOW FAMILY (Malvaceae)

D   VELVET LEAF, INDIAN MALLOW, PIE MAKER   *Abutilon theophrasti*

The yellow flowers are 1 inch (2.5 cm) wide and have numerous stamens. The fruit is a capsule with protruding beaks which was at one time used to pattern the edge of pie crusts. The plants are 3-6 feet (1-1.8 meters) high with large, heart-shaped leaves with a velvetlike surface. Native of India. Open areas, disturbed soils, gardens, roadsides, levees. Mainly recorded from across the northern part of the state, also in southeastern counties. July-October.

   A. incanum, Pelotazo, is a native species that is smaller. Found in 4 Ozark Region counties: Izard, Johnson, Newton, Stone. June-October.

A

B

C   D

A   FRINGED POPPY MALLOW   *Callirhoe digitata*

The wine-red or reddish-purple poppylike flowers are 2 inches (5 cm) wide and without bracts. The plants are 3-5 feet (1-1.5 meters) tall with very slender stems and few leaves. Erect, with the stems mostly glabrous. Dry, open areas, glades, roadsides. Ozark and Ouachita Mountain Region counties. May-August.

B   PURPLE POPPY MALLOW   *Callirhoe involucrata*

Flowers similar to those of the other *Callirhoe* species. Long, tapering sepals. A creeping plant with large leaves that have palmate, pointed lobes. Roadsides, open areas. Known mainly from a few Ozark Region counties. May-August.

C   POPPY MALLOW   *Callirhoe papaver* var. *bushii*

The flowers are similar to those of the above two species but larger. The petals may be straight-sided or rounded and overlapping. The lower leaves are broader than those of the other two species with broad lobes tapering to a point. An erect plant. Roadsides, open woods, edges of glades, valleys. Recorded in a few scattered Ozark Region counties. May-August.

D   ROSE MALLOW   *Hibiscus laevis*

The large reddish-pink or salmon-colored flowers have a darker colored area at the base of the petals and are several inches (cm) wide. Tall plants with leaves having lobed bases that are pointed. Edges of leaves with numerous small teeth. The leaves taper to a point. The shape of the leaves has suggested another name - Halberd-leaved Rose Mallow. This species is listed by many authors as *H. militaris*. Wet areas. Statewide. July-September.

A

B

C

D

A   ROSE MALLOW   *Hibiscus moscheutos* subsp. *lasiocarpus*

The white or rose-colored flowers are up to 6 inches (15 cm) across. There is a deep red or wine-purple area at the base of the petals. There are long hairs on the capsules. The plants are up to 7 feet (2. 1 meters) tall with slightly hairy leaves. Some leaves have 3- 5 shallow lobes or are heart-shaped. The seeds are eaten by quail and waterfowl. Wet areas. Statewide. July-September.

B   FLOWER-OF-AN-HOUR   *Hibiscus trionum*

The pale yellow flowers with a dark area at the base of the petals are 2-3 inches (5-7.5 cm) wide. Large yellow stamens. The plants are 1-2 feet (30-60 cm) high. A weedy plant that is native to Europe. Cultivated fields, gardens, idle land, roadsides. Known to occur in Pulaski, Jefferson, St. Francis and Washington counties. June-September.

C   CHEESES, COMMON MALLOW   *Malva neglecta*

The small flowers are lavender or white. The common name, Cheeses, is derived from the round, flat fruits. The leaves have 5-7 rounded palmate lobes and an indented base. The plants are low and creeping. Alien. Lawns, lots, idle ground. Found mainly in Ozark Region counties. April - September.

D   CAROLINA MALLOW   *Modiola caroliniana*

The orange, reddish-orange or purplish flowers are about ¹/₂ inch (13 mm) wide on slender stalks. There are 3 bracts below the calyx. The leaves have 6-7 toothed lobes. A low, creeping plant that roots at the nodes. Variety of sites including gardens, lawns, cultivated ground, disturbed soils. Southern counties. March-June.

A

B

C

D

A   SIDA   *Sida elliottii*

The deep yellow to nearly orange flat flowers are about ³/₄ inch (18mm) wide. The leaves are narrow on reddish stems. The plants are up to 3 feet (1 meter) high. Two other species of sida that occur in Arkansas are more weedy with small flowers. Usually in open areas, especially pastures. Reported from northeastern counties both in the Ozark and Delta regions, Crowley's Ridge. August- September.

ST. JOHN'S-WORT FAMILY (Hypericaceae)

B   ST. JOHN'S-WORT   *Hypericum spp.*

Most of these species have a thick, upright mass of stamens and bright yellow flowers. The leaf shapes vary considerably but in the larger species they are generally linear to oval. Some species have seeds that are taken by quail. Mainly plants of dry, open areas. Statewide. Summer into early fall.

   H. gentianoides, Pine Weed, Orange Grass, has small yellow flowers on the sides of or terminal on the branching slender stems with scalelike leaves. As the plant matures it becomes a reddish color. Grows on poor soils in open areas. Distributed over most of the state but seldom found in the Delta Region. *H. drummondii,* Nits-and-Lice, is similar with longer, slender leaves. Large, reddish seed pods. The flowers are terminal.

C   ST. ANDREWS CROSS   *Hypericum hypericoides*

A small shrub with yellow flowers having 4 narrow petals in the form of a slightly flattened cross, 2 large and 2 very small sepals, 2 styles, black seeds, fewer stamens than in most species of the genus. There is considerable variation in the height of the plants. Some are low and spreading, others upright, slender leaves, reddish stems. Various soils and sites. Statewide. July-September.

D   SHRUBBY ST. JOHN'S-WORT   *Hypericum prolificum*

A branching shrub with willowlike leaves and dark stems. The flowers often are in flat-topped groups with exceptionally thick masses of stamens in a dome-shaped arrangement. Well drained sites in hill areas. Found mainly in the western half of the state. June-September.

A

B

C

D

A ST. PETER'S-WORT   *Hypericum stans*

Similar to St. Andrew's Cross but with broader petals and veined sepals of unequal size, 3-4 styles and brown seeds. Numerous stamens. The leaves are large and nearly oval on the shrubby plants. Usually on sandy soils. Mainly in southwestern and southern counties. July-September.

B MARSH ST. JOHN'S-WORT   *Triadenum tubulosum*

The small pinkish flowers are about $^1/_4$ inch (6 mm) wide. The oblong leaves clasp the reddish stems and are light green to grayish-green. The seeds are eaten by ducks. Swamps, low, wet woods, around shady lakes and ponds. Scattered, probably more common than present records indicate. August- September.

ROCKROSE FAMILY (Cistaceae)

C SUN-ROSE, FROSTWEED   *Helianthemum carolinianum*

The bright yellow flowers are under 1 inch (2.5 cm) wide and last only a day, usually fading by noon, 3 broad sepals, 2 narrow ones. Hairy plants with thick roots. The upright stems bear oval leaves on plants that are seldom over 1 foot (30 cm) high. Open or shaded areas, sandy soils. A few southwestern counties, Jefferson County. April-May.

VIOLET FAMILY (Violaceae)

Violet plants are eaten by deer and in some species the seeds are taken by quail.

D GREEN VIOLET   *Hybanthus concolor*

This species has a different appearance than our other violets and can be recognized by the upright, dark green, pointed leaves on upright plants and the small, light green flowers hanging face-down from the leaf axils on slender, curved stems. The flower is somewhat violetlike with slender, equal length petals. One of these is broader and there is no spur. Hairy stems and leaf edges. The plants average 2 feet (60 cm) in height. Known mainly from Ozark Region counties. April-June.

A

B

C

D

A   CANADA VIOLET   *Viola canadensis*

The white petals have a purple tint on the backside. The flower stalks are slightly curved and there are small stipules. The center of the flower is yellowish. The branching stems are slightly purplish and somewhat hairy. The leaves are heart-shaped. Slopes, near ledges, rocky areas in woods. Central Ozark Region counties. April-May.

    V. striata, Pale Violet, Cream Violet, is similar but is usually found at lower elevations, such as along streams. The stipules are fringed or with the longer teeth up to 1/4 inch (1.5-5 mm) long. Mostly in mountainous counties.

B   WOOD VIOLET, WOOLLY BLUE VIOLET   *Viola sororia*

The deep violet flowers have bearded sidepetals; leaves and stems are hairy. The leaf shape is variable but is usually rounded. Variety of upland sites. Statewide. March-May.

    V. sagittata, Arrow-leaved Violet, has paler flowers and upright, lanceolate leaves that are notched at the base. Nearly statewide except for northeastern counties.

C   THREE-LOBED VIOLET   *Viola palmata*

Flowers similar to those of Wood Violet. The leaves have 3 to several lobes with the center one longest. Grows on a variety of sites but seems to prefer loose or sandy soils. Occurs statewide. March-May.

D   BIRD'S-FOOT VIOLET   *Viola pedata*

This violet occurs in at least three color phases: light, or dark violet, dark violet with 2 dark purple or "velvet" petals. The flowers are about 1 inch (2.5 cm) wide. The leaves are distinctive, being divided into very slender lobes suggestive of a bird's foot. These violets often cover large areas and are very showy. Sometimes eaten by deer. Hillsides, open woods, roadsides, often on thin soils. Over most of the state. Less common in the Delta Region. April-May. Sometimes in fall or winter in warm periods. Bloomed December 15, 1980 in western Little Rock.

A

B

C

D

A   YELLOW VIOLET   * Viola *pensylvanica*

Yellow flowers with the lower petal veined with purple. Heart-shaped leaves. Dry to low moist woods or streamsides. Mainly in the northwestern half of the state. April-May.

B   WHITE VIOLET   *Viola primulifolia*

The white flowers have purple veins in the lower petal. Flower stalks are reddish. Flowers are about $^1/_2$ inch (13 mm) wide. Leaves are oblong, somewhat pointed with slightly winged petioles near the base of the leaf blade. Damp areas, springs, steamsides. Well distributed in the Gulf Coastal Plain Region and southern Ouachita Mountain Region counties. March-May. Also in the fall.

V. lanceolata, Lance-leaved Violet, has white flowers and very narrow, usually upright leaves. In a few scattered counties.

C   JOHNNY-JUMP-UP   *Viola rafinesquii*

The small flowers are about $^1/_2$ inch (13 mm) wide and light to dark blue-violet in color with white or cream colored centers. The lower 3 petals are veined. This is a slender violet with dark colored stems. There is disagreement as to whether this is a native species. Fields, lots, roadsides. Statewide. March-May. Annual.

PASSION-FLOWER FAMILY (Passifloraceae)

D   PASSION FLOWER, MAYPOPS   *Passiflora incarnata*

These unique, fringed flowers are about 3 inches (7.5 cm) in diameter, purplish and white in color, sometimes all white. There are 5 drooping yellow stamens around the pistil which has 3-4 curved stigmas. The fruit or " maypop" is an elongated green berry that is often eaten by quail. The leaves are 3-lobed on a climbing vine with tendrils. Fencerows, roadsides, ditch banks, open areas. Statewide. May-September.

A

B

C

D

A   YELLOW PASSION FLOWER   *Passiflora lutea*

The flowers are not showy in this species but are fringed and about 1 inch (2.5 cm) wide, yellowish or yellowish-green in color. The leaves are 3-lobed with short blunt lobes. The tender shoots and tendrils are eaten by wild turkeys. Wooded areas. Nearly statewide. Blooms during May-July.

LOASA FAMILY (Loasaceae)

B   STICK LEAF   *Mentzelia oligosperma*

Yellow to yellow-orange flowers have numerous stamens and pointed petals. The leaves are an aid in identification being covered with hooked hairs, as are the fruits and stems, that cause them to adhere closely to clothes and the fur of animals. Stems and leaves are grayish-green, brittle. Rocky slopes, bluffs. Mainly in northern counties of the Ozark Region, Grant County. June-September.

CACTUS FAMILY (Cactaceae)

C   PRICKLY PEAR   *Opuntia compressa*

The showy large flowers are up to 3 inches (7.5 cm) across, yellow, often with orange to reddish centers, many stamens. The fruits are cone to pear-shaped and ripen to a reddish or purplish color. The fleshy "leaves" with spines are actually stems. Dry sites in openings, glades, banks, roadsides, old house places. Nearly statewide except for low, overflow areas. May-July.

LOOSESTRIFE FAMILY (Lythraceae)

D   TOOTH-CUP   *Ammannia coccinea*

The small reddish flowers are sessile in the axils of the leaves. There are 4 petals. The square stems and slender, linear, opposite leaves aid in recognizing this species. Plants are up to 2 feet (60 cm) high. Usually on damp ground near ditches, ponds, lakes, streams. Nearly statewide, less common in upland areas. June-September.

A

B

C

D

A   CLAMMY CUPHEA   *Cuphea viscosissima*

The small pink to reddish flowers have a tubular base and small petals, 2 above and 4 underneath. The opposite leaves are on reddish stems. The plants and flowers are covered with a sticky substance. Pastures, fields, roadsides. Ozark and Ouachita Mountain Region counties. July-October.

B   SWAMP LOOSESTRIFE   *Decodon verticillatus*

The pink flowers are in groups in the axils of the leaves on the upper parts of the long arching stems. Protruding stamens. A shrubby plant that may reach 8 feet (2.4 meters) in height. Leaves in pairs or threes. The seeds are eaten by ducks and the foliage by muskrats. Shallow water of lakes, swamps. Southern counties. July-August.

C   WINGED LOOSESTRIFE   *Lythrum alatum*

The small flowers are $\frac{1}{2}$ inch (13 mm) or less in width and vary in color from pale lavender to reddish-purple. The six petals are spread flatly on flowers carried singly in the leaf axils. As the plant matures the flowers become numerous along the stems. Spreading, upright stems. Lanceolate leaves are smaller toward the tops of the plants. The 4-sided stems may be slightly winged and reach 3 feet (1 meter) in height. Wet ground, ditches, prairies and roadsides. Nearly statewide. June-September.

    L. salicaria var. *salicaria*, Purple Loosestrife, has been discovered in Arkansas within the last few years. It is considered a pest species in most states since it may invade wetlands. It is a large plant with upright spikes of reddish-purple flowers. Alien.

MELASTOMA OR MEADOW BEAUTY FAMILY (Melastomataceae)

D   MARYLAND MEADOW BEAUTY   *Rhexia mariana*

The light pink to rose-colored flowers have 8, angled, prominent stamens, 4 flat irregular petals that are often recurved. Flowers are up to $1\frac{1}{2}$ inches (3.8 cm) wide. Pitcher or urn-shaped fruits are produced. The paired leaves are toothed and more narrow than those of Virginia Meadow Beauty. The stems are round and become woody and brown or reddish on the larger plants. Open areas, roadsides, railroads. Nearly statewide but not reported from several northern counties. June-early fall.

A

B

C

D

A VIRGINIA MEADOW BEAUTY   *Rhexia virginica*

Similar to the above but with darker flowers, wider, more rounded leaves. There are 4-sided, greenish, slightly winged stems on the larger plants. Lower, wetter areas. Occurrence is scattered over the lower two-thirds of the state. June-fall.

EVENING PRIMROSE FAMILY (Onagraceae)

B DEMAREE'S GAURA   *Gaura demareei*

White blossoms 1 inch (2.5 cm) wide or wider are most often in groups at the ends of the branches. The butterflylike flowers turn pink as they fade. There are 8 downcurved stamens. This species has flowers usually opening in morning hours. The tall plants up to 7 feet (2. 1 meters) high are much branched with small, pointed leaves. Discovered by Dr. Delzie Demaree. Roadsides, railroads, open areas. Southwestern counties, Franklin County. June-September.

C BIENNIAL GAURA   *Gaura longiflora*

Similar to Demaree's Gaura but with smaller flowers that are more evenly spaced over the branches. This species has flowers usually opening in the evening hours. Roadsides, open areas, old fields. Occurs statewide except for some of the Delta Region counties. June-September.

D SEEDBOX   *Ludwigia alternifolia*

The yellow flowers are small, about 1/2 inch (13 mm) wide, with large pointed sepals as long as the petals. Short, square pods with the sepals adhering form the "seed box." These turn reddish with age. The plants are up to 5 feet(1.5 meters) high with slender, alternate, pointed leaves that are willowlike. Wet roadside ditches, low open ground. Statewide. May-August.

L. decurrens also occurs statewide and can be separated from the above species by the presence of narrow wings or flanges on the stems that appear to be a continuation of leaf material downward on the stem. The stems are green.

A

B

C

D

A   FLOATING PRIMROSE WILLOW   *Ludwigia peploides*

The bright yellow flowers are about ¹/₂ inch (13 mm) wide. The vegetation consists of shiny green leaves on smooth, purplish stems that creep over muddy or shallow water areas, often rooting at the nodes. Mud flats, shallow water, ditches, pond edges. Scattered counties through the central part of the state, eastern and northeastern counties, Grand Prairie. June-October.

B   EVENING PRIMROSE   *Oenothera biennis*

The large yellow flowers, up to 2 inches (5 cm) across, open in late afternoon and close the next morning. Blooming occurs at the ends of the tall branches. The cross-shaped stigma and downcurved stamens are typical of this genus. The plants are often tall and branching, up to 8 feet (2.4 meters) high. Sometimes in thick stands. Dry, open areas. Statewide. June-September.

   Stenosiphon linifolius is a tall slender species with a long spike of small white flowers. When in bloom the leaves may be absent. It is not often seen since it is known from only 3 counties: Howard, Little River and Marion. It occurs on limestone glades. June-September.

C   SUNDROPS.   *Oenothera fruticosa*

Large, bright yellow flowers have petals that are noticeably veined. Flowers open during the day. Variable, slender, pointed leaves are smooth-edged. Plants 1-2 feet (30-60 cm) high. Dry soils, edges of woods, roadsides. Shade tolerant. Western half of the state. May-June.

D   CUT-LEAVED EVENING PRIMROSE   *Oenothera laciniata*

Small, light-yellow flowers turn reddish as they fade. The leaves are dandelionlike, incised. The plant is low growing or reclining with reddish stems. Often weedy. The seeds are often used for food by quail. Gardens, lawns, walks, curbsides, lots, fields. Statewide. April-frost.

A

B

C

D

A MISSOURI PRIMROSE *Oenothera missouriensis*

The very large, yellow flowers are about 4 inches (10 cm) wide and fade by midmorning on sunny days. During early morning hours the large petals are fully opened into a circular pattern and are extremely showy. The fruit is a large four-winged pod. Faded flowers turn dark. The plants are low-growing with narrow, willowlike leaves. Limestone glades, bluffs, roadsides. A few counties in the northern part of the Ozark Region. May-August.

B SHOWY EVENING PRIMROSE *Oenothera speciosa*

The white or pink flowers have yellow centers, pink veins and are about 2 inches (5 cm) wide. The fruit is an 8-ribbed capsule. Downy stems, wavy-edged leaves. Plants 1- 1¹/₂ feet (30-45 cm) high. Often in large roadside colonies. Easily grown, drought resistant. Dry open areas, roadsides, idle land, disturbed ground. Statewide. April-July.

GINSENG FAMILY (Araliaceae)

C GINSENG *Panax quinquefolius*

The tiny whitish flowers are in a rounded cluster at the end of a slender leafless stalk from the leaf axil. The berries are first green, later red. There are 3 large, 5-leaflet, toothed leaves on the low plants. This species is becoming scarce in some areas because of digging of roots for reported medicinal qualities. Rich woodland soils. Ozark Region counties, Crowley's Ridge. June-August.

CARROT OR PARSLEY FAMILY (Umbelliferae)

D HAIRY ANGELICA *Angelica venenosa*

The tiny white flowers are in compound umbels without bracts. Junction of the umbel stems with the flower stalk is red in color. The 3 leaflets often are divided further into 3's or 5's. The terminal leaflet is lobed. Edges of the leaflets are toothed. Stems are smooth and purplish-gray in the top part of the plants which are 4-5 feet (1.2-1.5 meters) tall. Open or shaded areas in woods, roadsides, streamsides. Northern part of the Ozark Region. June-August.

A

B

C

D

A SPOTTED COWBANE, WATER HEMLOCK *Cicuta maculata*

Tiny white flowers are carried in a loose umbel. The leaves are toothed and double or triple compound. The stems are streaked with purple. Tall plants 4-6 feet (1.2-1.8 meters) that are reported to be poisonous. The seeds are eaten by game birds. Wet pastures, fields, swampy areas. Statewide. June-September.

Conium maculatum, Poison Hemlock, is similar to Spotted Cowbane but with dark green, highly dissected fernlike leaves. Branching, hollow stems with purple spotting. Reported from a few extreme northwestern counties. Alien. May-August. *Ptilimnium nuttallii*, Mock Bishop's Weed, has tiny white flowers that are in slender- petioled rounded umbels. There are numerous threadlike bracts below the many rays of the inflorescense. The forked threadlike leaves on the short plants help identify this species. It usually grows in crowded stands seldom reaching 2 feet (60 cm) in height. Often fills ditches with a solid growth of plants. An annual. Both wet and dry sites, disturbed soils. Nearly statewide. May-August.

B WILD CARROT, QUEEN ANNE'S LACE *Daucus carota*

The tiny flowers are in tight umbels, white or occasionally tinged with pink. The central floret is sometimes purple in the mature umbel. The umbel is first concave, then flat and finally convex. As it fades it curls into a tight birdnest shape. Three pronged bracts are found below the flower heads. Basal leaves are formed the first year, flower stalks the second year (biennial). A branching plant with a large taproot and finely divided leaves. An ancestor of the cultivated carrot. Alien. Roadsides, idle fields. Statewide, less common in southeastern counties. May-frost.

C HARBINGER OF SPRING, PEPPER AND SALT *Erigenia bulbosa*

The small white flowers with reddish-brown anthers are in umbels. Plants are only 6-8 inches (15-20cm) high. The lobed leaves appear after the flowers. A round tuber grows at the lower end of the stalk. Rich woods, bottom of slopes, strearnsides. Ozark Region counties, Lee and Polk counties. February-April. One of the first flowers of spring. Survives cold weather while blooming.

D ERYNGO *Eryngium integrifolium*

The small, dense flower heads are bluish or purplish with slender, spiny bracts. Slender plants about 2 feet (60 cm) high are branching in the top part. Basal leaves have long petioles, are oblong and clasping. Very slender upper leaves. Wet sandy soils. Reported from Arkansas, Ashley, Calhoun and Union counties. August-October.

A

B

C

D

A   CREEPING ERYNGIUM   *Eryngium prostratum*

Creeping Eryngium has small purple flowers similar to those of Eryngo (above) on creeping, prostrate plants that occur over most of the state except for some of the northwestern counties. May-October.

B   RATTLESNAKE MASTER   *Eryngium yuccifolium*

The greenish, globe-shaped flower heads are 1 inch (2.5 cm) or less in diameter. The basal leaves are large, up to 2 feet (60 cm) long, and have spiny or bristly edges. Leaves often are blotched with brown. Upper stem leaves are clasping. Plants grow to 4 feet (1.2 meters) high. Dry, open ground. Statewide. June-August.

C   ANISE ROOT, SWEET ANISE   *Osmorhiza longistylis*

Tiny white flowers are grouped in small round umbels above the leaves. A hairy plant with wide, many-lobed leaves. All parts of the plant, expecially the roots, smell of anise or licorice. Leaves are hairy and triple compound. The lower leaves are often 1 foot (30 cm) or more in length. Plants are 3-4 feet (1-1.2 meters) high. Damp, woodland soils, valleys, along streams. Northern two-thirds of the state. April-June.

Torilis arvensis, Hedge Parsley, has small flat umbels on long stems well above the leaves. The seeds have hooked bristles and cling to clothing. The leaves have slender segments. The stems grow in a curved or zig-zag pattern and may reach 4 feet (1.2 meters) in height. Alien. Dry areas, roadsides, idle land, disturbed ground. Nearly statewide. Not reported from a number of southern counties. May-August.

D   COWBANE   *Oxypolis rigidior*

Tiny white flowers occur in umbels on angled stems. Leaves are compound and variable in shape, somewhat palmlike and dark green on the tall plants. The stems are hollow and smooth. Damp woodland soils, edges of woods and roadsides in moist soil, along streams. Primarily in northern Ozark Region and northern Ouachita Mountain Region counties. July-September.

A

B

C

D

A PRAIRIE PARSLEY   *Polytaenia nuttallii*

The light yellow flowers are in umbels. The lower leaves have flattened petioles that
sheath the stem. Upper leaves are nearly sessile on the upright plants that are up to 4
feet (1.2 meters) tall. There are leaflike bracts on the pedicels. Prairies, glades, open
areas. Scattered over most of the state. April-June.

   Thaspium trifoliatum, Meadow Parsnip and *Zizia aurea,* Golden Alexanders, have
similar flowers on smaller plants. In *Thaspium* the central flower in the umbellet is
stalked, in *Zizia* it is sessile.

WINTERGREEN FAMILY (Pyrolaceae)

The family is represented by only 2 species in the state.

B INDIAN PIPE   *Monotropa uniflora*

The flowers are white, yellowish-white or pink. There is only one flower per stalk;
these turn black with age. The seed pods are erect. Naked, scalelike leaves, fleshy
stalks. The plants seldom reach 1 foot (30 cm) in height. Woodlands. Scattered over the
state. September- frost.

   M. hyophithys, Pine Sap, has several nodding flowers per stem. These are reddish or
pale yellow. Reported from only a few western and central counties, also Craighead
County. Blooms during June-October.

HEATH FAMILY (Ericaceae)

C MOUNTAIN AZALEA   *Rhododendron prinophyllum*

Light to deep pink flowers appear before the leaves are fully developed. The flowers
are up to 2 inches (5 cm) wide. The leaves are oblong and pointed at each end. They
are hairy on the underside of the midrib. These shrubs are up to 6 feet (1. 8 meters)
high. Referred to as *R. roseum* by many authors. Regularly browsed by deer. Slopes,
valleys, along streams. Counties in the western half of the state. April-May.

PRIMROSE FAMILY (Primulaceae)

D SCARLET PIMPERNEL   *Anagallis arvensis*

The small flowers are $^1/_4$ inch (6 mm) wide and usually orange or red but may also be
white or blue. They are usually nodding on long slender stalks from the axils of the
opposite or whorled leaves and have long pointed sepals. The oval leaves are sessile on
the long stalks. Creeping plants less than 1 foot (30 cm) high. Alien. Roadsides, sandy
soil, idle land. Mainly in northwestern counties, reported also from Polk, Independence
and Randolph counties. June-August

A

B

C

D

A SHOOTING STAR   *Dodecatheon meadia*

The flowers are about 1 inch (2.5 cm) long and white, rose or lavender in color. The petals angle backward, 5 protruding stamens, erect seedpods. Lanceolate, basal leaves are usually upright around the long, bare flower stalk. Damp ledges and bluffs, prairies, slopes. Nearly all of the Ozark Region, also on the Grand Prairie and parts of the Ouachita Mountain Region. April-June.

B LOOSESTRIFE   *Lysimachia quadriflora*

The bright yellow flowers have rounded petals with a bristle at the tip. The petals overlap slightly at the base. Most of the flowers are borne at the tops of the plants and are about 1 inch (2.5 cm) across. The leaves are stiff, very slender and occur in whorls on the 1-3 foot (30-90 cm) high plants. Wet soils, along streams. Northeastern Ozark Region counties. July-August.

L. nummularia, Moneywort, is a creeping plant with paired, round leaves and yellow flowers about 1 inch (2.5 cm) wide. The petals have reddish dots. Grows in damp areas, along streams. Alien. Reported from a few northern and eastern counties. May-August.

LOGANIA FAMILY (Loganiaceae)

C YELLOW JESSAMINE   *Gelsemium sempervirens*

The yellow, trumpet-shaped flowers are 1½ inches (3.8 cm) long, fragrant and in clusters. Evergreen, smooth, lanceolate leaves are opposite on a climbing woody vine. Often cultivated. Eaten by deer in fall and winter. Woods, thickets, rocky areas or sandy soils. South Arkansas and a few central counties. February-May, occasionally in fall and winter.

D INDIAN-PINK   *Spigelia marilandica*

Bright red flowers with yellow interiors. These tubular flowers are 1½ inches (3.8 cm) long with 5 sharp lobes at right angles to the corolla. Leaves are opposite and sessile on plants about 2 feet (60 cm) tall. There are prominent leaf veins. Moist woods. Nearly statewide, less common in the Delta Region and northwestern Ozark Region counties. April-June.

A

B

C

D

GENTIAN FAMILY (Gentianaceae)

A   CATCHFLY GENTIAN, BLUEBELLS   *Eustoma exaltatum*

The large lavender flowers are 1½ inches (3.8 cm) in diameter with purple centers. Petals are united at the base into a short tube. Flowering is at the tops of the stalks. The opposite leaves are about 3 inches (7.5 cm) in length, oblong, glaucous, and clasp the stem. The vegetation is light green in color. Plants grow to 3 feet (90 cm) tall. This species was recently discovered in several sizeable colonies along the Arkansas River in Jefferson County. River banks, possible prairies. Scattered central and southeastern counties. May-October.

B   DOWNY GENTIAN   *Gentiana puberulenta*

Five-petaled flowers without fringes are funnel-shaped, dark purple. The petals are more separate than in other Arkansas gentians. Opposite, lanceolate leaves and stems with a fine downy covering (pubescent). Prairies, glades, bluffs, slopes. Known from Benton, Washington, Saline and Prairie counties. September-October.
*   *G. flavida,* Pale Gentian, is a pale colored gentian with flowers similar in form to those of Soapwort Gentian, except that they open at the tips. The plants grow 1½ to 2 feet (45-60 cm) high. Found in a few northern Ozark Region counties, Logan and Yell counties. Blooms during August-October. *G. quinquefolia, Stiff Gentian, has flowers that are small and tube-shaped, lilac in color with 5 lobes tipped with bristles. They measure about 1 inch (2.5 cm) or less in length and are borne in tight groups. The stems are 4-angled. Reported from a few central Ozark Region counties. August-November.

C   SOAPWORT GENTIAN   *Gentiana saponaria*

The blue to nearly purple flowers remain closed or may open slightly. Erect sepals occur at the base of the egg-shaped blooms. Plants are up to about 2 feet (60 cm) high with a soapy juice. Moist woods, sandy open areas. Central counties, also reported from Union and Washington counties. September- November.

D   FLOATING HEART   *Nymphoides peltata*

The yellow flowers have petals that are delicate near the edges. The flowers are about 1½ inches (3.8 cm) wide and grow on a bare pedicel up to 4 inches (10 cm) long. The leaves are 2-3 inches (5-7.5 cm) in diameter and nearly round. An introduced species. Ponds, lakes, etc. Known from Benton and Washington counties only. July-September.

A

B

C

D

A   PENNYWORT   *Obolaria virginica*

The flowers are about ¹/₂ inch(13 mm) long, white and usually in groups of 3. There are 4 petals, joined in the lower half and 2 sepals. Low plants with thick stems and leaves. Moist hardwood or hardwood-beech forest. Known only from Cross and St. Francis counties on Crowley's Ridge. March-May.

B   ROSE PINK   *Sabatia angularis*

The bright pink flowers are up to 1 inch (2.5 cm) wide with yellow centers and protruding, forked styles. Sometimes white flowers are found. Paired flowering branches have 4-angled stems and broad opposite leaves. A biennial plant up to 3 feet (1 meter) tall with clasping leaves, winged stems. Pinelands, rocky areas, roadsides. Statewide. June-August.

S. brachiata, Marsh Pink, is without clasping leaves. The lower stems are rounded. This species has been found on the Grand Prairie and in several other counties in the eastern part of the state. *S. campestris* has 4 angled stems that are not winged and large calyx lobes extending nearly to the ends of the petals. Occurs in a belt of counties across the state from northwest to southeast.

C   AMERICAN COLUMBO   * *Swertia caroliniensis*

The 4-petaled flowers are about 1 inch (2.5 cm) wide with brownish-purple dots and a large gland on each petal. The tall plants are up to 8 feet (2.4 meters) high and have whorls of leaves at regular intervals up the stalk when in bloom. The basal leaves are very large, up to 1¹/₂ feet (45 cm) long and lanceolate in shape. Plants may have only basal leaves for several years and then die after blooming. Often found in large colonies. Stream valleys, low woodlands in hill counties, pastures and other open areas. Scattered central and northeastern counties. June-July.

DOGBANE FAMILY (Apocynaceae)

D   BLUE STAR   *Amsonia ciliata*

The light blue flowers are in dense groups well above the very slender linear leaves. The star shape is distinctive. The blooms are about ¹/₂ inch (13 mm) wide. Roadsides, open areas. Found in northcentral and westcentral counties. April-June.

A. tabernaemontana, Blue Star, has sky-blue, star-shaped flowers in thick, rounded groups at the tops of the stems. Leafy plants with a milky juice, often occuring in thick colonies. The leaves are lanceolate to nearly linear with a dull upper surface. This is the most common of the 3-4 species of blue star in the state. Roadsides, bluffs, along streams. Statewide. April-June.

A

C

D

B

A   INDIAN HEMP, DOGBANE   *Apocynum cannabinum*

The small white flowers are only ¹/₃ inch (8 mm) long in close groups near the tops of the plants and are bell-shaped and upright. The long, slender seed pods are in pairs, slightly curved and 4-6 inches (10-15 cm) long. The shrublike plants are 3 feet (1 meter) or more in height with reddish stems and upright leaves with white midribs. The plants have a milky juice, The tough bark has been used for making rope. Dry areas such as roadsides, fields, woodland edges, prairies. Nearly statewide. June-August.

B   COMMON PERIWINKLE   *Vinca minor*

The blue flowers, up to 1 inch (2.5 cm) wide, are borne singly in the leaf axils. Funnel-shaped corollas with white star-shaped central markings. Trailing, evergreen, ivylike plants that have escaped from cultivation. Native of Europe. Old house places, edges of woods and thickets, shaded areas. Scattered locations over the state. March-June.

MILKWEED FAMILY (Asclepiadaceae)

The genus *Asclepias* contains the upright milkweed plants with milky juice, seeds with silky fibers in large pods, and flowers with reflexed lobes that make them appear as if they were wearing skirts. Flowers in umbels.

C   CURLY MILKWEED   *Asclepias amplexicaulis*

The crown of the flower is purplish. The corolla is olive to brownish-green. Curved flower stems (pedicels) give the plant a windblown appearance. Opposite sessile leaves. Plant height variable depending upon the site. Open woods, hillsides, roadsides. Often on thin or bare soils. Scattered over most of the state west of the Delta Region. May-July.

D   PURPLE MILKWEED   *Asclepias purpurascens*

The reddish-purple flowers are carried on stiff stalks. Leaves with reddish veins, downy underneath. Plants are about 3-4 feet (1-1.2 meters) high when fully grown. Rocky ground, roadsides, open areas. Mainly in northern counties, also in a few southern counties, Pulaski County. May-July.

A

B

C

D

A   FOUR-LEAVED MILKWEED   *Asclepias quadrifolia*

The flowers are usually white, sometimes pinkish or lavender. Leaves in the central part of the plant are in whorls of 4, thus the name. A slender plant 12-18 inches (30-45 cm) tall. Woodlands, along roads and trails. Shade tolerant. Ozark and Ouachita Mountain regions into the northern Gulf Coastal Plain Region. April-July.

B   BUTTERFLY WEED   *Asclepias tuberosa*

The bright orange or reddish-orange flowers, rarely yellow, are very attractive to butterflies. A thick root. The juice is not milky in this species. Open areas, disturbed soil. Nearly statewide, less frequent in the Delta Region. May-September.

C   WHITE-FLOWERED MILKWEED   *Asclepias variegata*

The white flowers have purple central markings. Erect, purplish stems up to 3 feet (1 meter) high. Leaves with yellowish veins. Roadsides, woodland openings, idle ground. Nearly statewide, not known from extreme northwestern counties. May-July.

D   GREEN-FLOWERED MILKWEED, SPIDER MILKWEED   *Asclepias viridis*

The large flowers are green with purplish crowns and are in cupped bracts. Plants usually in round clumps. The thick leaves are on stems that may droop or recline. Prairies, glades, pastures, limestone areas. Scattered locations in all regions of the state. April-September.

A

B

C

D

A   GREEN MILKWEED   *Asclepias hirtella*

Slender, green flowers and slender, linear leaves. Prairies, roadsides, glades. In scattered counties over the state but not known from the Delta Region outside of the Grand Prairie. May-August.

MORNING GLORY FAMILY (Convolvulaceae)

Some of the species furnish seeds that are taken by quail.

B   HEDGE BINDWEED   * *Convolvulus sepium*

The usually white or lavender tinted funnel-shaped flowers are 2-3 inches (5-7.5 cm) long with 2 bracts enclosing the calyx. The arrowhead- shaped leaves have blunt lobes at the base. A climbing vine with creeping, pulpy roots, often weedy. Some forms of this species are introduced. River banks, fencerows, idle land, fields. Northern counties. May-September.

C. arvensis is smaller, white or pink, without bracts and usually grows low along the ground. Scattered throughout the state.

C   RED MORNING GLORY   *Ipomoea coccinea*

Small red flowers with orange centers. Heart-shaped leaves. Native of South America. Disturbed ground, especially in fields, gardens. Northern counties, Polk County are recorded locations. June-September.

D   BLUE MORNING GLORY, IVY-LEAF MORNING GLORY *Ipomoea hederacea*

Flowers up to $1\frac{1}{2}$ inches (3.8 cm) wide are blue or sometimes purplish, rarely pink or white. Leaves are 3-lobed. Fields, gardens, open areas. Statewide. June-October.

I. purpurea, Common Morning Glory, is native to tropical America but has become naturalized in a few northwestern counties, Craighead, Polk counties and probably others that have not been reported. It occurs in a variety of showy colors particularly reds and purples. July-October.

172

A

B

C

D

A   WILD POTATO VINE   *Ipomoea pandurata*

Can be identified by the large white trumpet-shaped flowers with a purple area at the base of the throat. The flowers usually fade by mid-day. Heart-shaped leaves. The large fleshy root may weigh several pounds. Fencerows, roadsides, idle lands. Statewide. May-September.

B   TIE VINE   *Jacquemontia tamnifolia*

The small blue flowers are about $\frac{1}{2}$ inch (13 mm) wide and in dense groups with very hairy sepals. Flowers are on long stems. A twining vine that often becomes a pest in crops and gardens. Oval leaves 4-6 inches (10-15 cm) long. Fields, roadsides, idle land, gardens. South Arkansas, Polk County. July-frost.

PHLOX FAMILY (Polemoniaceae)

Species in the genus *Phlox* are often difficult to identify because of intergrading characteristics.

C   SAND PHLOX   *Phlox bifida*

The flowers are light purple or lavender to nearly white, about $\frac{2}{3}$ inch (16 mm) across with V-shaped notches in the ends of the petals. These little plants form thick mats several feet in diameter. The leaves are slender and light green in color. Various parts of the plant have gland-tipped hairs. Several varieties have been described within the species but there is disagreement as to their validity. Rocky slopes, road cuts, ledges, often on limestone soils. Northern counties. March-May.

D   BLUE PHLOX, SWEET WILLIAM   *Phlox divaricata*

Varying shades of blue or lavender, light pink to nearly white flowers are about $\frac{3}{4}$ inch (18 mm) wide in loose clusters. They spread from the tip of the stalk. Opposite, pointed stem leaves are smooth. The stem is slightly hairy and sticky. Plants are about 1 foot (30 cm) tall. Sterile shoots from the base of the plant often root at the joints. Strearnsides, wooded slopes, edges and openings. Statewide. April-June.
P. drummondii, Annual Phlox, is often cultivated and may escape in sandy soils. It is a western species. The low plants have flowers in many patterns of red and white, also other colors. April-August.

A

B

C

D

A   SMOOTH PHLOX   *Phlox glaberrima*

The bright pink or "hot-pink" flowers are closely spaced in a globular inflorescence and have broad sepals and an almost cylindrical calyx. Plant parts are smooth, without hairs, slender, with narrow, pointed leaves. Prairies, low areas in woods, along roadsides. Mainly in eastern and southern counties. May-June.

P. paniculata, Garden Phlox or Perennial Phlox, is a commonly cultivated species. A stout plant with broad leaves that have lateral veins and usually purplish-pink flowers. Grows to about 5 feet (1.5 meters) tall with a single stalk. Usually found along streams. Northern Arkansas is part of the natural range. It has become naturalized elsewhere in the state. June-October.

B   DOWNY PHLOX   *Phlox pilosa*

The flowers are most often pink or pale pink, sometimes white with purple centers. The stamens are entirely within the corolla. The plants are slightly hairy or downy. The leaves are slender, dark green and opposite. Dry areas, thin soils, rocky or shale outcroppings, openings in woods. Statewide. April-July.

C   JACOB'S LADDER   *Polemonium reptans*

The light blue to violet-blue, bell-shaped flowers have protruding yellow stamens. Individual flowers in the terminal clusters are about ¾ inch (18 mm) wide. A drooping plant with pinnately compound leaves in which the leaflets are at right angles to the main stem, ladderlike. Moist slopes, benches, streamsides in wooded areas. Mainly in northern Arkansas but scattered elsewhere. April-May.

WATERLEAF FAMILY (Hydrophyllaceae)

D   BLUE WATERLEAF   *Hydrolea ovata*

The showy, deep blue or royal-blue flowers at the tops of the stems are about 1 inch (2.5 cm) in diameter with very prominent whitish stamens. Hairy foliage with spiny stems makes handling difficult. An erect, stout plant usually growing in dense stands that when in full bloom appear as a bright blue blanket. Wet ground or shallow water, road ditches, near ponds, lakes. In nearly all counties but seldom reported from the Ozark Region. July-September.

A

B

C

D

A WATERLEAF, HYDROLEA   *Hydrolea uniflora*

The small blue, bell-shaped flowers grow along the sides of the stems. The plants are not hairy but are armed with spines at the base of the petioles. The leaves are slender. Wet woods, ditches, etc. Nearly statewide except for hill counties with higher elevations. June-September.

B WOOLEN BREECHES   *Hydrophyllum appendiculatum*

The lavender flowers are about ¹/₂ inch (13 mm) in diameter in groups at the top of the plants. The blossoms have greenish centers and prominent stamens with dark anthers. The plants are hairy and 1-2 feet (30-60 cm) tall. A biennial with maplelike leaves. Rich woods, slopes, valleys. Northcentral Ozark Region counties, also Franklin County. April-July.

C VIRGINIA WATERLEAF   *Hydrophyllum virginianum*

The violet to nearly white flowers are in round clusters on long stems above the leaves. They are bell-shaped with stamens extending well beyond the petals. Leaves are up to 5 inches (12.5 cm) long with 5-7 sharply toothed leaflets which often are splotched and stained in appearance. Plants are 1-2 feet (30-60 cm) high. Woodlands. A few Ozark Region counties. April-July.

D BABY BLUE-EYES   *Nemophila phacelioides*

Blue flowers 1-1¹/₂ inches (2.5-3.8 cm) in diameter have a large whitish area in the center. The broad petals are slightly notched at the tips. These weak-stemmed plants are sprawling with leaves having 3-7 sharp pointed lobes; these with a few large, pointed teeth. Edges of woods, low areas, roadsides, along streams. Western counties. May-July.

A

B

C

D

A HAIRY PHACELIA   *Phacelia hirsuta*

The light blue or lavender flowers are in clusters along an unfolding flower stalk at the tops of the plants. Prominent stamens have hairy filaments, calyx hairy, corolla to ³/₄ inches (18 mm) wide. The plants are hairy and up to 1 foot (30 cm) tall. Leaves are pinnately divided with the upper leaves sessile. Damp areas, roadsides, slopes. Nearly statewide, less frequent in the eastern counties, April-May.

BORAGE or FORGET-ME-NOT FAMILY (Boraginaceae)

B   WILD COMFREY, GIANT FORGET-ME-NOT   *Cynoglossum virginianum*

Small flowers ¹/₂ inch (13 mm) wide are on tall, usually forked flower stalks and are light blue to nearly white. The leaves are clasping on the hairy stems. The basal leaves are very large, hairy, stalked, and in a rosette. Plants are 2-2¹/₂ feet (60-75 cm) tall. Shaded woodlands, edges, slopes. Statewide but less frequent in southernmost counties. April-June.

C   BLUE-WEED, VIPER'S BUGLOSS   *Echium vulgare*

The blue flowers have long upper lips and protruding red stamens. The flowers bloom one or two at a time on the curled flower stalks and are ³/₄ inch (18 mm) long. An upright plant with bristles on the stems and leaves. This plant is considered weedy, and may be extending its range. Grows to 3 feet (1 meter) high with slender pointed leaves. Native of Europe. Idle land, open areas, roadsides, gravel bars. Reported from a few northwestern counties but may become more commonly found. May-September.

D   INDIAN HELIOTROPE, TURNSOLE   *Heliotropium indicum*

The small flowers are in a curved, pointed inflorescence and are pale blue with orange centers. Inflorescence is curved at first, becoming longer and straighter. Plants are erect, up to 3 feet (1 meter) tall with thick stems and leaves, often weedy. Alien. Variety of sites. Statewide. June-frost.

A

B

C

D

A   HELIOTROPE   *Heliotropium tenellum*

This species has an entirely different appearance than the preceding one although in the same genus. The flowers are white, flat and are borne at the ends of the branches. The stems and leaves are very slender, hairy, and the height is usually 1 foot (30 cm) or less. Drought resistant, often in large colonies on rocky ground. Seems to prefer limestone or dolomite soils, open areas. Northern Ozark Region counties, southwestern counties on calcareous soils. June-August.

B   ORANGE PUCCOON   *Lithospermum canescens*

Orange-yellow flowers at the tops of the many branches are tubelike at the base flaring out into flat faces with rounded petals. The flowers are about $^1/_2$ inch (13 mm) in diameter. The plants are covered with fine white hairs, have oblong leaves and are up to about 1 foot (30 cm) tall. Rocky or sandy soils, dry areas, slopes, glades. Well distributed over the northern half of the state except for the Delta Region, also in a few southwestern counties. April-June.

    L. caroliniense is a larger plant with yellow flowers and very narrow leaves that occurs in southwestern counties. *L. incisum* can be recognized by the fringed, crinkled edges of the petals and yellow flowers. It has been recorded in Washington and Sebastian counties. *L. arvense*, Corn Gromwell, and *L. latifolium* are white flowered species with very small flowers; the first is fairly well distributed and has much narrower leaves.

C   BLUEBELLS   *Mertensia virginica*

Blue, trumpet or bell-shaped flowers about 1 inch (2.5 cm) long hang in clusters. Moist woodlands. Northern Ozark Region. March-June.

VERVAIN FAMILY (Verbenaceae)

D   FOG FRUIT   *Phyla lanceolata*

The very small white flowers are in rounded clusters at the tops of long, bare peduncles. Blossoms are in a ring around the knoblike heads. The leaves are lanceolate to oblong and slightly toothed near the tips. A creeping plant that may occur in large colonies. Adapted to various soils along streams, idle land, city lots and sidewalk areas. The seeds are eaten by waterfowl. Over most of the state. May-September.

A

B

C

D

A   DAKOTA VERVAIN   *Verbena bipinnatifida*

The small rose or lavender flowers are in thick clusters. This species can be recognized by the fernlike, finely divided leaves and hairy stem. The stems often are reclining. Seems to prefer calcareous soils, open sites. A few southwestern counties. May-September.

B   BRAZILIAN VERVAIN   *Verbena brasiliensis*

Small, star-shaped, violet flowers grow on pulpy, cylindrical heads. Tall plants up to 7 feet (2.1 meters) high with straight, erect, square stems. Alien. Sandy soils, open areas, idle land. Mainly in southern Arkansas. Appears to be extending its range. June-September.

C   ROSE VERVAIN   *Verbena canadensis*

This is probably the best known species of verbena in the state. The rose-colored flowers in rounded clusters are about ¹/₂ inch (13 mm) wide with notched petals and a short corolla tube. Calyx about half as long as the tube. Leaves are distinctive with double toothed, cleft lobes. Low, bushy, hairy plants less than 2 feet (60 cm) high, often growing in thick clumps. Easily cultivated. Vervain fruits are a preferred turkey food in some areas. Sandy or rocky soils, roadsides, pastures, slopes, other open areas. Nearly statewide, but not often seen in the Delta Region. March- September. Our earliest verbena.

D   HOARY VERVAIN   *Verbena stricta*

The small blue to purplish flowers, rarely white, are on straight spikes that are arranged in candelabra fashion above the leaves. Sturdy plants up to 4 feet (1.2 meters) high with oval, toothed leaves having very short petioles. Leaves and stems are hoary with fine white hairs. Open areas, idle fields, roadsides, pastures and barn lots, often on thin soil. In nearly all counties across the northern third of the state, also in a few central counties. June-September.

V. simplex, Narrow-leaved Vervain, is like a small version of the above species with slender stems and leaves and grows to about 2 feet (60 cm) tall. It usually has pale blue to white flowers and is very common along roads in many northern counties of the Ozark Region. May-September.

A

B

C

D

MINT FAMILY (Labiatae)

A OHIO HORSE MINT   *Blephilia ciliata*

Small, bluish, lavender or nearly white flowers grow in a ring around the flower head.
These are stacked one above the other in pagoda fashion, up to 7 on each stalk, and
measure about 1½ inches (3.8 cm) in diameter. The plants are 2-3 feet (60-90 cm) high
with nearly stalkless leaves. Woodlands. Mainly in Ozark Region counties, Crowley's
Ridge, Polk County. May-July.

B DITTANY   *Cunila origanoides*

The pinkish, lavender, or nearly white flowers are small and in clusters or tufts from
the axils of the leaves and tips of the branches. The 2 long stamens and the forked pistil
protrude. The reddish steins are stiff, wiry and numerous. The leaves are opposite,
sessile and oval with pointed tips. The plants are only about 1 foot (30 cm) high and
have a strong mint odor. Dry areas, woodlands or roadsides. Nearly statewide, not
reported from some southern and southeastern counties. July-October.

  Hedeoma pulegioides, Pennyroyal and *H. hispida*, Mock Pennyroyal, are somewhat
similar but smaller plants with bluish flowers in the axils of the opposite leaves. The
plants are erect and aromatic, especially *H. pulegioides* which is late blooming. Both
occur nearly statewide.

C HENBIT   *Lamium amplexicaule*

The purplish or rarely, white, erect flowers are in the axils of the upper leaves which
are rounded, sessile and encircle the stem. Plants are 4-10 inches (10-25 cm) high when
in bloom. Alien. Nearly all open areas, especially idle land, fields, lawns, road
shoulders. A common lawn flower. Statewide. February-May, sometimes in fall or
winter. Blooms very early in open areas.

D DEAD NETTLE   *Lamium purpureum*

Flowers are similar to those of Henbit but lighter in color. The upper leaves may vary
in color with shades of gold, reddish-yellow and purple and are slightly pointed, often
drooping. Alien. Roadsides, openings, fields, lawns. Scattered over the state. March-
September.

A

B

C

D

A   MOTHERWORT   *Leonurus cardiaca*

The small lavender flowers surround the stalks just above the bases of the leaves. The long, horizontal or drooping leaves with 3 large lobes are distinctive. The plants grow to 5 feet (1.5 meters) high. Alien. River banks, open woods, idle land. Reported from only a few Ozark Region counties. June-August.

B   BEEBALM, WILD BERGAMOT   *Monarda fistulosa*

The flowers are pinkish, lavender or lilac. This is the most common species of the *Monarda* genus of horsemints. Plants are 2-4 feet (60 cm-1.2 meters) high when in bloom. These are browsed by deer. Roadsides or other openings, disturbed ground, Statewide. June-September.

M. stipitatoglandulosa resembles the above species but has white flowers. It is found in central Ouachita Mountain Region counties.

C   DOTTED MONARDA   *Monarda punctata*

The yellow flowers are dotted with round purplish spots. The bracts below the flowers are whitish, lilac or reddish-purple. Roadsides, woodland openings, cutovers, rocky or sandy ground. Mainly reported from southwestern Arkansas, northcentral and northwestern counties. June-September.

M. citriodora, Lemon Mint, has flowers that are usually pink or whitish with purplish spots. Occurrence is very scattered in the state.

D   HORSEMINT   *Monarda russeliana*

The white flowers with purplish dots are in a circular flower head. The plants grow to about 2 feet (60 cm) in height. Rocky or sandy soils, well-drained sites in open or partially shaded woodlands. Northern and central counties. April-June.

M. bradburiana is very similar and some botanists treat the two as one species. This species is described as having a shorter corolla.

A

B

C

D

A   FALSE DRAGONHEAD, OBEDIENT PLANT   *Physostegia virginiana*

The nearly white to reddish-purple flowers often are numerous and closely spaced in long spikes. The showy flowers somewhat resemble a dragon's head in shape and are about 1 inch (2.5 cm) in length. The plants are 3 feet (1 meter) or more in height. Lanceolate, toothed leaves. Moist open areas, streambanks, ditches, roadsides, prairies. Nearly statewide. Not reported from most southwestern counties. April-August.

B   SELF-HEAL, HEAL-ALL   *Prunella vulgaris*

The purple and white flowers bloom first from the bottom and later from the tops of square to cylindrical flower heads which are located at the ends of the stalks. The lower lip of the flower is fringed. The pointed leaves often angle downward and are finely lobed. Sometimes found in thick stands and grows to about 1$^1/_2$ feet (45 cm) high. Alien. Idle land, roadsides, open areas. Statewide. May-August.

C   MOUNTAIN MINT   *Pycnanthemum albescens*

The white flowers have small purple dots. The leaflike bracts beneath the flowers are whitish-green, appearing frosted. The leaves are whitish underneath. Plants are up to 4 feet (1.2 meters) tall. Dry soils along roads and railroads, other open areas. Statewide. June-August.

D   SLENDER MOUNTAIN MINT   *Pycnanthemum tenuifolium*

The small white or lavender flowers are in rounded heads at the tops of the plants and are lightly spotted. There are many stems. The leaves have very slender segments. Plants grow to about 3 feet (1 meter) high. Woodland edges, openings, roadsides. Statewide. June-August.

A

B

C

D

A   BLUE SAGE   *Salvia azurea*

The light blue or sky blue flowers are on terminal spikes or in the axils of the upper leaves. The lower lip is very large and nearly flat. Flowers are up to 1 inch (2.5 cm) long. Tall plants up to 5 feet (1.5 meters) high with slender, linear to lanceolate leaves that are opposite. No basal leaves. Roadsides, glades, fields and pastures, other open areas or partially shaded edges. Found mainly in the western half of the state. June-October.

B   CANCER WEED, LYRE-LEAVED SAGE   *Salvia lyrata*

Light blue to violet flowers about 1 inch (2.5 cm) long are in whorled groups at the tops of the stalks. Leaves are mostly basal and deeply indented into rounded lobes with the tip segment being the largest. The leaves often have purplish areas or are edged with purple. Plants are 1-2 feet (30-60 cm) high. On almost any type of open or partially shaded ground. Statewide. April-June.

C   CALAMINT   *Satureja arkansana*

The small lavender and white flowers have 3-lobed white lower lips. Flowers are borne over most of the plant. The leaves are slender and opposite, not numerous. The plants have a strong mint odor. Open rocky areas, glades, ledges. Most of the Ozark Region counties, a few Ouachita Mountain Region counties. May-August.

D   HAIRY SKULLCAP   *Scutellaria elliptica*

The pale blue to violet flowers are borne in an upright position closer to the stalks than in most species in the genus. Later the flower stalks elongate. Oval to lanceolate leaves are in pairs at wide intervals and are more scalloped than toothed. A hairy plant. Skullcaps are a preferred deer food. Woodlands, partially shaded areas. Most of the Ozark Region counties, a few of the Ouachita Mountain Region counties. May-August.

A

B

C

D

A   ROUGH SKULLCAP, HYSSOP SKULLCAP   *Scutellaria integrifolia*

Purplish flowers with 2 white central markings. The leaves are slender and not toothed or scalloped. There are small slender leaves in the axils. Openings, often in thick vegetation, edges. Commonest in southern counties. May-July.

B   HEART-LEAVED SKULLCAP   *Scutellaria ovata*

Purple flowers with white lower lips are in spikes at the tops of the plants and measure nearly 1 inch (2.5 cm) long. The calyx is humped on the underside. Leaves are often heart-shaped but also may lack the indentation at the base. The leaf edges are roughly toothed. The stems and undersides of the leaves are hairy. The plants are large, up to $2^{1}/_{2}$ feet (75 cm) high. Open woodlands, edges, roadsides in timbered areas, often abundant in disturbed ground such as cutovers. Widespread in the Ozark and Ouachita Mountain regions. April-May.

C   WOOD SAGE, GERMANDER   *Teucrium canadense*

The lavender to pinkish flowers are in a terminal inflorescence that is spikelike. Individual flowers are $^{3}/_{4}$ inch (18 mm) long with 4 protruding stamens. The lower lip is so large as to make the flower appear 1-lipped. The stems and undersides of the leaves are hairy. These are large, sturdy plants which in later stages have a much elongated flower "spike." Dry or moist sites along roads, railroads, edges of lakes, disturbed soil. Statewide. June-August.

In *Stachys* spp. the upper and lower lip positions are widely separated. The flowers are in the axils of the leaves but these become so closely spaced in the top part of the plants that the appearance is of a spike. The leaf shapes and the amount of hairyness is variable. Some species grow to 3 feet (1 meter) or so in height. Found in low areas nearly statewide. The blooming period is June-September.

D   FORKED BLUE CURLS   *Trichostema dichotomum*

The blue and white flowers have 4 long, curled, protruding stamens. The lower lip is drooping and spotted. The flowers are $^{3}/_{4}$ inch (18 mm) long in pairs or 3's at the ends of the stems. The plants have spreading branches, opposite leaves, square stems and are about 2 feet (60 cm) high. Along streams, fields, often in dry or sandy soils. Scattered over the western half of the state. August-September. Annual.

A

B

C

D

NIGHTSHADE FAMILY (Solanaceae)

A   JIMSON WEED   *Datura stramonium*

The long, trumpet-shaped flowers are usually pale lilac with deeper colors near the base. The fruit is an egg-shaped spiny capsule. Flowers are up to 5 inches (12.5 cm) long. The large, alternate leaves have large teeth and are on purplish stems. This plant has a disagreeable odor. The plants grow to 5 feet (1.5 meters) high. Alien. Pastures, fields, lots. A pest in croplands. Statewide. June-October.

Physalis is a genus in which the identification of individual species is often very difficult because the characteristics by which they are separated are variable.

B   GROUND CHERRY   *Physalis pumila*

The flowers are yellow to greenish-yellow with fine-lined brown central markings. The flowers usually hang face downward, are bell-shaped and about 3/4 inches (18 mm) wide. A yellow round berry somewhat resembling a tomato is produced inside a papery, lanternlike calyx. The leaves have rounded bases with few teeth to none. The stems have sticky hairs. The plants are up to 2 feet (60 cm) high and have forked or branching hairs on the stems and leaves. The fruits are eaten by turkeys and quail. Dry woods, openings. Mainly in northwestern Arkansas. May-September.

C   HORSE NETTLE, BULL NETTLE   *Solanum carolinense*

The white flowers are about 1 inch (2.5 cm) wide and have recurved petals that are joined at the base. The petals are occasionally purplish. The yellow centers are formed by the large stamens. The fruit resembles a small tomato and is green at first, later turning yellowish. The leaves have large, irregular teeth and the stems are brownish with sharp spines. Plants may grow to 2-3 feet (60-90 cm) high. Fields, pastures, idle land. Often a troublesome weed. Statewide. May-October.

D   BUFFALO BUR   *Solanum rostratum*

The yellow flowers are about 1 inch (2.5 cm) in width. The fruit is a round, spined berry or "bur." The stems and leaves have very sharp spines. The leaves are crinkled with many rounded lobes. Idle land, roadsides, often in thin soils, disturbed soils. More frequent in northern counties. May-October.

A

B

C

D

FIGWORT OR SNAPDRAGON FAMILY (Scrophulariaceae)

The genus *Gerardia*, used by many authors, is a complicated group. For purposes of clarity here, the genus *Gerardia* is split with the pink-flowered species placed in *Agalinis* and the yellow-flowered species in *Aureolaria.*

A GERARDIA   *Agalinis fasciculata*

The pink to reddish-purple flowers are among the deepest colored of those in the genus. The interiors are light in color with dots of the petal color. The white stamens are noticeable. The flowers are bell-shaped and about 1 inch (2.5 cm) in length. The plant grows to about 3 feet (1 meter) in height with very narrow, unlobed leaves. There are groups of small leaves in the axils on the lower part of the plants. The pedicels are not longer than the calyx and the stems have upright hairs. Parasitic upon roots of grasses and other herbaceous plants. Roadsides, idle land. Most common in the lower three-fourths of the state. July-September.

B YELLOW FALSE FOXGLOVE   *Aureolaria flava*

Large, yellow, bell-shaped flowers $^3/_4$ inch (18 mm) wide and about $1^1/_2$ inches (3.8 cm) long are carried near the ends of the branches. The stems in this species are smooth and without hairs (glabrous). The leaves are opposite, and in the top part of the plant, narrow and without lobes. The large leaves in the middle and lower part of the plant are lobed - dandelion fashion. Open woods, roadsides, usually near oaks (reported to be parasitic upon oak roots.). Northern half of the state and into the southcentral counties. June-October.

C FERN-LEAVED FALSE FOXGLOVE   **Aureolaria pedicularia*

The yellow flowers are about $1^1/_2$ inches (3.8 cm) long. The stems and leaves are hairy. The leaves are fernlike. Rocky and sandy soils, dry open areas, road banks, glades. Scattered, mainly in the Ozark and Ouachita Mountain regions. July-September.

D BLUE HEARTS   *Buchnera americana*

Flat, purplish, phloxlike flowers are located along the top part of the stalk and measure $^1/_2$ inch (13 mm) across. The buds are at the tips of the stalks. When pressed and dried the blossoms and other plant parts turn black. The stalk is unbranched, hairy and grows to about 2 feet (60 cm) tall. The leaves are 3-veined. Prairies, idle land, thin woods. On the Grand Prairie and other scattered prairies, open areas. June-September.

A

B

C

D

A INDIAN PAINTBRUSH   *Castilleja coccinea*

The flowers are small and inconspicuous. It is the upturned bracts surrounding the flowers that are a brilliant orange-red or sometimes yellow. The leaves and bracts have 3 narrow lobes. The plants are 1-2 feet (30-60 cm) high. A very adaptable species growing in the tight, acid soil of the Grand Prairie and on rocky, alkaline, limestone hillsides of the Ozark Region. Widely scattered over the state but usually on prairies. Less frequent in the northeastern and southwestern counties. April-June. Annual or biennial.

B TURTLEHEAD   *Chelone glabra*

The white or pinkish flowers are solitary or in a dense group of several blossoms with the pointed buds at the top. The tubular flowers are somewhat flattened along the sides. This is a perennial species having opposite leaves with short petioles. The leaves are long, slender and evenly toothed. Moist woods, along streams. Apparently limited to a few locations in extreme northeast Arkansas. August-October.

C VIOLET COLLINSIA   *Collinsia violacea*

A two-colored flower with the upper lobes white and the lower a rich violet. The flowers are about $1/2$ inch (13 mm) long and usually in whorls. The central segment of the lower lip is folded around the stamens and style and is nearly hidden. The leaves are short-stalked or sessile and opposite on plants that average about 1 foot (30 cm) high or less. Roadsides, open woods, glades. Northwestern counties make up the main range of the species in Arkansas. April-June.

C. verna, Blue-eyed Mary, has blue lower lobes and is known from Benton, Carroll and Newton counties. This species is widespread in central Missouri.

D BLUE TOADFLAX   *Linaria canadensis*

Flowers about $1^1/2$ inch (13 mm) long are light shades of blue with a downcurving spur nearly as long as the flower. The flower stalk continues to elongate with the flowers blooming near the top. The leaves are linear and shiny in the middle and upper part of the plant. The basal leaves are oval. Old fields, fallow ground, burned or open woods, roadsides, disturbed ground. Often becomes abundant under favorable conditions. Statewide. April-September.

Kickxia elatine, Cancer Root, has small flowers with a spur. The lower petals are purple and yellow. Leaves triangular. A creeping plant of streams, gravel bars and low areas. Native of Europe. Northern counties and a few western counties. June-October.

A

B

D

C

A BUTTER AND EGGS   *Linaria vulgaris*

The yellow and orange flowers have a spur and are about 1 inch (2.5 cm) long. The leaves are slender and grayish-green on plants up to 2 feet (60 cm) high. Native of Europe. A pest in some states to the north. Dry areas, garden spots, idle land. Northern Ozark Region counties. May-October.

B MAZUS   *Mazus japonicus*

Although small, $^{1}/_{4}$-$^{1}/_{2}$ inches (6-13 mm) long, the flowers are attractive at close range. The upper lip is blue or lavender and the 3-parted lower lip is lighter with a raised whitish area covered with yellow dots. The leaves are oval, slightly toothed and are mainly found in the lower part of the plant. A creeping vine of open areas. A native of Asia that is sometimes cultivated. Lawns, gardens, sandy soils. Southeastern half of the state. Probably not well reported because of its size. July-October.

C   MONKEY FLOWER   *Mimulus alatus*

The blue or lavender to nearly white flowers are about 1 inch (2.5 cm) long with the 2 lobes of the upper lip erect, like a pair of ears. The flowers have short stalks. The leaves are opposite and stalked on the square stems. The plants grow to about 5 feet (1.5 meters) tall. Damp areas both open and shaded. Statewide but not common on Delta Region soils. June-September.

M. floribundus, Yellow Monkey Flower, is found in several counties of the Ozark Region. *M. ringens* has violet flowers on long stalks, the leaves are sessile. It has been reported from Baxter and Fulton counties.

D   LOUSEWORT, WOOD BETONY   *Pedicularis canadensis*

The flowers are greenish-yellow or reddish-purple and in dense whorls at the top of the flower stalks. The top lip is longer and overhangs the lower. The leaves are oblong with regular, prominent teeth and have a fernlike appearance. The plants are up to 1 foot (30 cm) high. Along streams, open woods, slopes. Statewide but less frequent in the Delta Region. April-May.

Parentucellia viscosa has yellow flowers with 3 lobes on the broad lower lip. This species has recently been discovered in Franklin and Jefferson counties. It is a native of Europe.

A

B

C

D

Penstemon, beard-tongue, species have one of the stamens bearded and one sterile. Nine species have been recorded in the state.

A ARKANSAS BEARD-TONGUE   *Penstemon arkansanus*

Whitish flowers with lavender streaking average ³/₄ inch (18 mm) in length. The lower half of the stem is somewhat hairy. There are usually several stems per plant and these are purplish. The leaves are dark green and may be smooth or have fine hairs. Plants are usually less than 2 feet (60 cm) high. Rocky open woodlands, roadsides, glades. Well distributed in the western two-thirds of the state. April-June.
   P. laxiflorus is a similarly colored species with larger flowers hanging in loose clusters and occurs in the southern quarter of the state. April-May.

B PURPLE BEARD-TONGUE   *Penstemon cobaea*

This species is easily identified by the size of the flowers: up to 2 inches (5 cm) long and nearly 1 inch (2.5 cm) in diameter. The most common color is purple but reddish-purple or nearly white flowers occur. The leaves are downy and clasp the stems, which grow to about 2 feet (60 cm) tall. Bluffs, ledges, prairies, roadsides. Prefers calcareous soils. Northcentral Ozark Region counties and 3 southwestern counties - Hempstead, Little River and Sevier. April-June.

C FOXGLOVE BEARD-TONGUE   *Penstemon digitalis*

Crisp white flowers have almost equal length petal lobes at the end of the funnel-shaped corolla which is about 1 inch (2.5 cm) in length, dark stamens. The flower stalks are in pairs and are slightly hairy. The plants are up to 4 feet (1.2 meters) tall. Open areas, fields, roadsides. Statewide. May-July.
   P. tubiflorus is similar but the flower face is flat and the flowers are grouped more closely around the stalk. Somewhat more northern in distribution.

D RED PENSTEMON   *Penstemon murrayanus*

An easily recognized species with bright red flowers. The plants are tall, up to 6 feet (1.8 meters) high, with cupped, sessile leaves. The stems are reddish. Open sandy ground. Recorded in Nevada and Ouachita counties. More common in states west of Arkansas. May-June.

A

B

C

D

A   MULLEIN FOXGLOVE   ** Seymeria macrophylla*

The yellow flowers are woolly or hairy inside the corolla. The plants are tall, up to 6 feet (1.8 meters) high on fertile soils and have spreading branches that angle upward. There are two leaf shapes; the upper leaves are lanceolate and not lobed, the lower leaves are larger, pinnately lobed and toothed. A preferred deer food but seldom found in quantity. Moist woodlands, shady areas, valleys, thickets. Mainly in the Ozark Region. Recorded also from two Gulf Coastal Plain counties and Woodruff County. June-September.

B   MOTH MULLEIN   *Verbascum blattaria*

Yellow and white flowered forms occur. The central area of the flower is reddish-brown. Flowers are in long, open spikes and each is about $^{3}/_{4}$ inch (18 mm) wide. The clasping leaves decrease in size in the top part of the plants which often reach 5 feet (1.5 meters) in height. Alien. Pastures, idle land, fields, roadsides, open woods, especially in burned or disturbed areas. Nearly statewide. Few reports from the southernmost counties. May-September.

C   WOOLLY MULLEIN   *Verbascum thapsus*

Small, cupped, yellow flowers are borne on tall, thick stalks. The large, woolly leaves are grayish-green. The leaves in the basal rosette are largest. The stem leaves are progressively smaller up the straight stalks. A native of Europe. Dry, open areas of all types, disturbed soils. Statewide. May-September.

D   SPEEDWELL   *Veronica* spp.

These small flowers are seen most often in lawns, yards, fields and similar open areas. Most are blue with dark blue veins in the petals and have white centers. The plants are low-growing, often with oval, toothed leaves. A total of 8 species has been collected in the state. Some are alien. Statewide. February-August.

A

C

B

D

A   CULVER'S ROOT   *Veronicastrum virginicum*

The long, densely- flowered, sharp-pointed spikes of tiny white flowers are distinctive. The plants are up to 5 feet (1.5 meters) tall with evenly spaced whorls of leaves on the stalks. Widely adapted to various soils, open or wooded sites. Nearly all reports have been from the northern half of the state and the Grand Prairie. June-September.

TRUMPET CREEPER FAMILY (Bignoniaceae)

B   CROSS-VINE   *Bignonia capreolata*

The dark-red tubular flowers have flaring lobes that are yellow on the inside. The flowers are in clusters and each is about $1^1/_2$ inches (3.8 cm) long. The plant is a woody vine with leaflets in pairs about 4 inches (10 cm) long. The plant climbs by means of tendrils. A cross can be seen in a cross section of the stem. Woods, thickets. Nearly statewide but not reported from about 15 northwestern counties. April-June.

C   TRUMPET CREEPER   *Campsis radicans*

Reddish-orange, trumpet-shaped flowers are 3 inches (7.5 cm) long in a flaring cluster. The leaves are compound with many-toothed leaflets. The vines are climbing and often reach well up into trees and other objects. Heavily browsed by deer in spring and summer. Nearly all soils, openings, fencerows, idle land, railroads, roadsides. Statewide. May-August.

BROOMRAPE FAMILY (Orobanchaceae)

Two species of this family occur in Arkansas.

D   BEECH DROPS   *Epifagus virginiana*

The small, inconspicuous flowers are streaked with white and lavender. The flowers are tubular, opening into sharp lobes.The lower flowers do not open. The plants are low and much branched with brownish stems and scalelike "leaves." Even from a short distance the plants appear to be groups of dead steins. Under or near beech trees where it "feeds" upon the trees' roots. Central Ozark and Ouachita Mountain Region counties, the Gulf Coastal Plain Region and Crowley's Ridge. September-October.

A

B

C

D

A ONE-FLOWERED CANCER-ROOT *Orobanche uniflora*

The white to pale lavender, single blossom is at the top of the slender, leafless stalk. The petals are lightly veined on flowers about ³/₄ inch (18 cm) long. The plants seldom reach 1 foot (30 cm) in height and have brownish scales near the base instead of leaves. Parasitic. The plants are usually found in groups. Moist woodlands, slopes. Collected from only a few widely scattered counties. April-June.

BLADDERWORT FAMILY (Lentibulariaceae)

Utricularia is the only genus from this family that occurs in the state. Four species have been collected or reported from a limited number of counties. These plants are so small that they are probably being overlooked by collectors.

B CONE-SPUR BLADDERWORT *Utricularia gibba*

The bright yellow flowers are borne on slender, bare stalks and have a short spur. The corolla is only about ¹/₃ inch (8 mm) wide and there are usually one or two flowers on each 2-4 inch (5- 10 cm) stalk. There are threadlike runners under the water or on the bottom. These bear hairlike segments which are actually leaves. Shallow, quiet waters or boggy areas. In widely scattered counties over the state. May-September.

U. subulata has one to several flowers on each slender purplish stalk. The stalks are up to 6 inches (15 cm) high. The lower lip of the flower is much broader than the upper. There is a flat spur against the upper lip. The small rounded leaves are at the bottom of the stalks. Damp sandy soils, boggy areas. Reported from Benton, Drew and Union counties. April-August.

C FLOATING BLADDERWORT *Utricularia inflata*

The flowers are about ¹/₂ inch (13 mm) wide and 2-lipped, somewhat pealike in form. This aquatic species floats by means of radiating, inflated branches. There are submerged, hairlike much-branched leaves which bear tiny bladders that trap minute forms of aquatic life. The plants are usually less than 8 inches (20 cm) high. Lakes, ponds, etc. Known from Lake Maumelle in Pulaski County and a few other localities at this time. May-June.

ACANTHUS FAMILY (Acanthaceae)

D DICLIPTERA *Dicliptera brachiata*

The narrow, 2-lipped flowers are pink to reddish-purple and about ³/₄ inch (18 mm) long. There are 2 stamens. The plants average 2 feet (60 cm) high with oval, somewhat pointed leaves. Along streams, other damp areas. Scattered counties in the Ozark and Ouachita Mountain regions, a few counties in the north part of the Gulf Coastal Plain Region. July-October.

A

B

C

D

A WATER WILLOW   *Justicia americana*

The pale violet, white or lavender flowers have a design of darker shading in the center. The flowers are ³/₄ inch (18 mm) across with the lower part 3-lobed, 2 stamens. Flowers are not noticeable from a distance because of the thick foliage. They are in dense round clusters. Long, slender, willowlike leaves. Plants are often in thick stands in shallow water. Grows to 2¹/₂ feet (75 cm) tall. Streams, gravel bars, ditches, edges of lakes. Common throughout the Ozark and Ouachita Mountain regions and in a few Gulf Coastal Plain Region areas. May-September.

   J. ovata has smaller more uniformly colored lavender flowers scattered along the peduncle, oval-shaped leaves and is more of a lowland species distributed over the southeastern half of the state. May-July.

B SMOOTH PETUNIA   *Ruellia strepens*

The violet flowers have dark veins in the petals and arise from the leaf axils. They grow to nearly 2 inches (5 cm) long. The stems and opposite leaves are smooth. The flowers are on stalks about the length of the flower that bear 2 small leaves. Plants are usually 2 feet (60 cm) tall or less. Used regularly as food by deer. Open woods, glades, roadsides, prairies. Statewide. May-October.

   R. humilis, Hairy Petunia, has similar flowers but hairy stems and leaves. The flowers and leaves are nearly sessile. The leaves are sharp pointed, opposite and usually upturned. Statewide. May-October.

LOPSEED FAMILY (Phrymaceae)

Only one species from this family occurs in the state.

C LOPSEED   *Phryma leptostachya*

The small pink and white flowers have long lower lips that are white and 3-lobed. The pink upper lip is recurved. The flowers are at right angles to the stem. As the fruit develops, it and the calyx turn downward, parallel to the stem. Woodlands. Scattered over the entire state. June-September.

PLANTAIN FAMIILY (Plantaginaceae)

The genus *Plantago*, Plantain, has 9 recorded species in the state. All except *P. lanceolata*, have inconspicuous flowers. This is the only genus within the family that occurs in the state.

D ENGLISH PLANTAIN   *Plantago lanceolata*

Tiny white flowers bloom in a ring around the cylindrical, pulpy head. The heads are on the ends of long, slender, bare stalks up to 3 feet (1 meter) tall. The leaves are long and narrow in a basal rosette. A native of Europe. Dry areas, along roads, streets, idle land, fields. Statewide. April-October.

A

B

C

D

BEDSTRAW or MADDER FAMILY (Rubiaceae)

A   BUTTONWEED   *Diodia virginiana*

Small, white, 4-petaled flowers less than ½ inch (13 mm) wide have united corollas below the petal lobes and are carried in the leaf axils. A creeping plant which roots at the nodes and is often weedy. The leaves are opposite and narrow on square stems. Moist or dry open areas, lawns, ditches, near water or low areas. Statewide. June-October.

    D. teres, Poor Joe, has lavender flowers, square stems and is an upright, weedy plant of fields and idle land. Statewide. June-September. Seeds of both the above species are important quail and turkey foods.

Hedyotis, including *Houstonia*, is the genus of bluets which are small plants with small 4-lobed flowers. These are attractive in spite of their size and often the bluets will cover the ground with a blue or white blanket of color. A total of 10 species of *Hedyotis* is recorded for Arkansas. The seeds of some species furnish quail food.

B   BLUET   *Hedyotis caerulea*

White to blue, 4-lobed flowers with yellow centers are nearly ½ inch (13 mm) wide and often grow thickly in stands several feet wide. The lobes may be veined with a darker blue. Low plants with very slender stems not over 6 inches (15 mm) high. The basal leaves are oblong, about ½ inch (13 mm) in length and opposite. Open road shoulders, idle fields, open areas in woodlands. Counties through the central part of the state from north to south. April-June.

C   STAR VIOLET, BLUETS   *Hedyotis crassifolia*

The white to nearly purple flowers are very small, usually less than ¼ inch (6 mm) wide and on threadlike stems. This is the most common species in lawns and other such open areas. There are small oval leaves at the base of the plant. The plants are 4 inches (10 cm) or less in height. Lawns, pastures, road shoulders, fields. Statewide. February-April.

    H. australis, Least Bluets, has white flowers that are only half as large as those of the above species. Absent from many northern and northeastern counties.

D   LONG-LEAVED BLUETS   *Hedyotis longifolia*

The white to lavender flowers are less than ¼ inch (6 mm) wide. The flowers are in 2's or 3's at the ends of the stems. The leaves are slender and in pairs. The plants are less than 1 foot (30 mm) high. Dry areas, open woods, glades. Nearly statewide but not reported for several southern counties. May-September.

A

B

C

D

A   MOUNTAIN HOUSTONIA, LARGE HOUSTONIA   *Hedyotis purpurea*

The white to pale violet flowers are in wide, terminal groups. The leaves are fairly large, oval, paired and sessile with 3 noticeable veins. This is a large species and may grow to over 1 foot (30 cm) high, appearing as a small rounded shrub. Rocky or sandy soils in open woods or other open to partly shaded areas. Nearly statewide but seldom reported from northeastern or southwestern counties. May-June.

B   PARTRIDGE BERRY   *Mitchella repens*

Small, white, hairy flowers are usually in pairs at the ends of the stems. A red berry is produced with 2 scars from the double flowers. These are sometimes eaten by quail. The stems are creeping and lie close to the ground with paired, rounded leaves that are evergreen and dark in color with noticeable veins. Moist woodland sites. Over most of the central and southern part of the state. May-June.

HONEYSUCKLE FAMILY (Caprifoliaceae)

C   YELLOW HONEYSUCKLE   *Lonicera flava*

Yellow blossoms that turn red as they age are about 1 inch (2.5 cm) long. The woody vines climb or trail along the ground and have opposite, sessile leaves that are oval. Slopes, rocky ledges, roadsides, woodlands. Mainly recorded in Ozark and Ouachita Mountain Region counties, also in a few Gulf Coastal Plain Region counties. April-May.

D   JAPANESE HONEYSUCKLE   *Lonicera japonica*

The yellow and white blossoms produce round, blue-black berries. Strong, woody vines climb on other vegetation or may cover large areas as a ground cover. A weedy plant in many areas but considered an important deer browse plant by wildlife managers. Native of Asia. Adapted to nearly all types of areas. Statewide. May-July, but also to some extent in other months.

A

B

C

D

A   TRUMPET HONEYSUCKLE   *Lonicera sempervirens*

Long, red, tubular flowers with the inside of the lobes yellow. The rounded leaves circle around the stem (perfoliate). Escaped from cultivated plants. Slopes, open or shaded woodlands, along streams, thickets. Nearly statewide, less frequent in northeastern counties. April-July.

B   HORSE GENTIAN   *Triosteum perfoliatum*

The reddish, curved, tubular flowers have slightly flaring lobes and are in a whorl around the stem in the axils of the leaves. Yellowish stamens protrude from the $^3/_4$ inch (18 mm) long flowers which have long, pointed bristly sepals. The large, long leaves are opposite and perfoliate on the sticky stems. The leaves grow up to 10 inches (25 cm) long on plants that average 3 feet (1 meter) in height. Open, dry or rocky areas, woodland openings. Mainly in scattered Ozark and Ouachita Mountain Region counties. May-July.

T. angustifolium, Yellow-Flowered Horse Gentian, has yellow flowers. The leaves are 2 inches (5 cm) long. It occurs in northern counties and also has been reported from a few eastern and southern counties.

VALERIAN FAMILY (Valerianaceae)

C   CORN SALAD   *Valerianella longiflora*

Numerous small white flowers are in flat-topped clusters on pedicels from the axils of the leaves. The buds are purplish. The upper stems are usually purplish. The leaves are in pairs, opposite and spatulate to oblong, Often found in large stands of closely grouped plants. Plants are usually less than 1 foot (30 cm) high. Open glades or rocky areas, open woods, roadsides. Westcentral counties. April-June.

D   CORN SALAD   *Valerianella radiata*

The small white flowers are in square or rectangular clusters that occur in pairs or 4's at the end of the upper branches. The branching stems are in pairs that fork just above the opposite, irregularly toothed clasping leaves in the upper part of the plants. The plants are up to 2 feet (60 cm) high. The lower leaves are broader and spatulate. Open ground, idle land, fields, roadsides. Statewide. April-June.

A

B

C

D

TEASEL FAMILY (Dipsacaceae)

Teasel is the only species from the family in Arkansas.

A   TEASEL   *Dipsacus fullonum*

The tiny lavender flowers bloom in a ring around the egg-shaped, spiny flower head. Long upward curving bracts emerge from below the head. Blooming begins in the center of the head and then progresses upward and downward. The fruiting head of this species has been used in industry to "comb" the nap of woolen cloth. Long leaves up to 1 foot (30 cm) in length are opposite and pointed. Native of Europe. Roadsides, fencerows, barnlots, pastures, idle ground, along railroads. Northwestern Ozark Region counties, Polk County. June-September.

BELLFLOWER FAMILY (Campanulaceae)

B   TALL BELLFLOWER   *Campanula americana*

Deep blue or violet-blue flowers with a white circle in the center and a long, curved style are distinctive. The flowers are 1 inch (2.5 cm) or more in width and open at various points along the stalk rather than in sequence. The plants are tall, 4-6 feet (1.2-1.8 meters) high and have slender leaves. Easily grown from seed. Shade tolerant. The leaves are browsed by deer. Stream banks, ledges, slopes, woodlands. In the majority of the counties in the northern two-thirds of the state. June-September.

The genus *Lobelia* is represented by 6 species in the state.

C   CARDINAL FLOWER   *Lobelia cardinalis*

There is a thick spike of cardinal-red flowers. The stamens protrude from the top part of the flower and are white tipped. The plants average about 3 feet (1 meter) tall. Near water or moist areas, ditches, streams, edges of lakes, springs. Shade tolerant. Statewide. August-October.

D   GREAT BLUE LOBELIA   *Lobelia siphilitica*

Large blue flowers are 1 inch (2.5 cm) long or longer with white stripes underneath the lower lip and pointed, hairy calyx lobes. Large plants up to 3 feet (1 meter) high. Deer eat the leaves of this species. Moist areas in woodlands, along streams, gravel bars, springs, roadside ditches. Ozark Region, Crowley's Ridge, a few Ouachita Mountain Region counties. July-October.

A

B

C

D

A   LOBELIA, HIGHBELIA *Lobelia spicata*

The blue to pale blue flowers are $^1\!/_2$ inch (13 mm) or less in length. The two upper lobes are stiffly erect and usually recurved. Flowers are in long, slender spikes. The plants are usually 3 feet (1 meter) or less in height with leaves that are not toothed. The stems are often reddish. Variety of sites. Nearly statewide, less frequent in low areas and in the Delta Region. May-July.

    L. appendiculata, has similar flowers but the leaves have small sharp teeth. April-June. *L. inflata* has very small, slender, light-blue flowers and the calyx becomes inflated and round as the fruit develops. Both of these species are fairly well distributed over the state. June-August. *L. puberula*, Downy Lobelia, Big Blue Lobelia, has large flowers without striping underneath and they usually are along one side of the stem. The plant has a fine down over the vegetative parts. The leaves are ovate and toothed. Damp areas over most of the state except for northern counties. August-October.

B   CHICKEN SPIKE *Sphenoclea zeylandica*

The white to pale violet flowers are small with short, rounded lobes and are borne in dense spikes somewhat resembling a small green pine cone. The plants grow to 4 feet (1.2 meters) tall with thick, oblong leaves. Alien. Moist areas. Central and eastern counties. August-October.

C   VENUS' LOOKING GLASS *Triodanis perfoliata*

Bluish-purple, star-shaped flowers about $^3\!/_4$ inch (18 mm) wide arise from the leaf axils along the stem. The leaves are cupped, rounded, and clasp the stem. The plants grow 1-2 feet (30-60 cm) high and are single stalked. Quail sometimes feed upon the seeds of this plant. Nearly any type of open ground, often on poor soils. Statewide. April-August.

A

B

C

COMPOSITE or SUNFLOWER FAMILY (Compositae)
EARLY COMPOSITES

A   PUSSY'S TOES   **Antennaria plantaginifolia*

The fuzzy, white to greenish-white flower heads are rounded and terminal on the short stalks. Male and female flowers usually are on separate plants. The short plants, 10 inches (25 cm) or less in height, are woolly with spatulate leaves in a basal rosette. The stalk leaves are narrow, pointed and sessile. The basal leaves have 3-5 parallel, prominent veins and are a preferred deer food in fall and winter months. Usually on dry sites and poor soils, often in open woodlands. Statewide. April-June.

B   MAYWEED, DOG-FENNEL   *Anthemus cotula*

The white and yellow daisylike flower head has a dome-shaped disk. The heads are up to 1 inch (2.5 cm) wide with a chafflike material among the disk flowers. The plants have finely divided leaves and a strong, bitter odor and taste. Often grows in rounded clumps. Alien. Pastures, idle land, fields, roadsides, barn lots. Scattered over the state. April-October.

C   PHILADELPHIA FLEABANE   *Erigeron philadelphicus*

The white to pink ray flowers are numerous on flower heads that average $^3/_4$ inch (18 mm) wide. The basal leaves are hairy and toothed, up to 6 inches (15 cm) in length and oblong. The smaller stem leaves are clasping. The plants measure 1-3 feet (30-90 cm) high with soft stems. Browsed by deer. Open areas, fields, lawns. Statewide. April-July.

E. pulchellas, Robin's Plantain, has flower heads that are usually solitary on the upright hairy stems and are about 1 inch (2.5 cm) across. The rays may be white or lilac. This species has runners at ground level and is shorter than other species in the genus. It is distributed statewide and blooms during April-June.

D   WOOLLY RAGWORT   *Senecio tomentosus*

The yellow flower heads are on slender, dark colored stems. The leaves have long slender petioles and are lanceolate with densely packed, whitish, woolly hairs on the undersurface and on the stems. The plants are 1-2 feet (30-60 cm) high. Roadsides, open woods, other open areas. Nearly statewide except for some northwestern counties. April-June.

A

B

C

D

LATE COMPOSITES

A ASTER *Aster anomalus*

Small flower heads about $1/2$ inch (13 mm) in diameter have bluish rays and yellow to reddish disks depending upon the age of the bloom. The lower leaves are lanceolate with indented or heart-shaped bases. The upper leaves are short and linear. Most of the leaves, especially the lower ones, have petioles. In this species the leaves are without teeth. Asters are regularly used as deer browse in spring and summer months. Dry roadsides, open woods or idle land. Mainly in the northwestern half of the state. August-November.

B WHITE HEATH ASTER *Aster pilosus*

The flower heads are $1/2$-$3/4$ inch (13- 18 mm) wide with white rays and yellow disks and are numerous along the branches. The leaves are narrow and sessile on plants up to 5 feet (1.5 meters) tall. Widespread on dry, open sites. Nearly statewide, but not recorded from the Grand Prairie. August- December. This is the latest blooming white aster that occurs throughout the state.

C TICKSEED SUNFLOWER *Bidens aristosa*

The flower heads with yellow ray and disk flowers average about $1 1/2$ inches (3.8 cm) wide. The 2-pronged seed-pods adhere to clothing and the fur of animals. The leaves are opposite, up to 6 inches (15 cm) long, and pinnately divided into several toothed segments. The plants have numerous branches and are often found in large, thick stands. Plants grow to 6 feet (1.8 meters) tall. Damp or dry sites along roads, idle fields, ditches, disturbed ground. Statewide. August-November. One of two extremely late-blooming, yellow composites. The other is described below.

D NARROW-LEAVED SUNFLOWER *Helianthus angustifolius*

The large flower heads are about 2 inches (5 cm) in diameter with yellow rays and a dark brown disk. The flowers may be closely grouped on low plants or well spaced on the upright, taller plants. The plants may reach 7 feet (2.1 meters) in height and have very narrow leaves up to $1/4$ inch (6 mm) wide and 4-6 inches (10-15 cm) long. Roadsides, fields, pastures, idle land, woodland openings, ditches. Records show the range to be in the lower three-fourths of the state and on Crowley's Ridge. August-November. This is the state's latest blooming, dark-centered yellow composite.

A

B

C

D

OTHER COMPOSITES

A COMMON MILFOIL, YARROW   *Achillea millefolium*

The small, individual flower heads in the flat-topped clusters are about ¼ inch (6 mm) long. The ray flowers are white, grayish or rarely pink and the central or disk flowers are pale yellow. Dried flowers are used in arrangements, often dyed. There are cultivated forms in various colors. The fernlike leaves are unusual in this family. The plants usually grow in clumps and have a pungent odor. Average height is 2½ feet (75 cm). Native of Europe. Railroads, idle ground, old fields. Statewide. May-August.

B COMMON BURDOCK   *Arctium minus*

The pink or lavender and white, rounded, bristly flower heads are about ¾ inches (18 mm) wide. The individual flowers are tubular. There are numerous, slender, hooked bracts around the entire head. The lower leaves are heart-shaped on the hollow stalks. The plants are 3-5 feet (1-1.5 meters) high. Alien. Pastures, idle land. Mainly in northern counties, also reported from Polk County. July-October.

Aster is a large genus with over 20 recorded species in Arkansas. Every county has at least a few species. The disk flowers are yellow and the ray flowers are white or various shades of blue, lavender, etc. Identification of individual species is sometimes difficult. The flowers, seeds and leaves of a number of species of aster are used for food by deer and game birds.

C ASTER   *Aster paludosus* subsp. *hemisphericus*

The large, daisy-type flower heads are 1-2 inches (2.5-5 cm) wide and nearly sessile on the stems with sharp-pointed leaves under them that extend past the rays. The stems are unbranched with long, slender leaves up to 6 inches (15 cm) long and less than ½ inch (13 mm) wide. There is a woody corm at ground level that is tuberlike. The plants are 1-2 feet (30-60 cm) high. Sandy to rocky soils, open areas. Mainly in the southern half of the state. August-October.

   A. patens, Spreading Aster, has flowers that are similar but smaller on widely spreading branches. The leaves are short and blunt with bases that nearly encircle the stem. Statewide. The blooming period is August- November.

D SILKY ASTER   *Aster sericeus*

The violet to bluish-purple rays are somewhat downcurved and the flowers are usually terminal on the spreading branches. The leaves are broad in proportion to the length and sessile, with a pointed end and blunt base. A noticeable feature is the silvery-gray, silky appearance of the leaves. Glades, rocky slopes. Known in Arkansas only from the Devil's Knob-Devil's Backbone Natural Area in Izard County at this time. This species is well distributed in southern Missouri. August-October.

228

A

B

D

C

A   WESTERN DAISY   *Astranthium integrifolium*

The small flower heads are flat with rays that are light blue or pink near the ends and white near the disk. The plants seldom exceed a foot (30 cm) in height with leaves that are short, slender and slightly wider near the tips. This is the only species of the genus in this part of the United States. An aid in identification is the early blooming period as compared to most composites. Found on rocky or sandy soils in open areas, glades or along streams or more shaded sites. Occurs throughout most of the Ozark and Ouachita Mountain Regions. March-June.

B   BERLANDIERA   *Berlandiera texana*

This species is unusual in that the disk is greenish. The yellow rays are notched at the ends and have the appearance of having been attached to the flower head rather than growing out of it. The leaves are alternate along the stems, usually grouped near the base of the plant, oblong to lanceolate, and evenly toothed. Rocky areas, openings in woods, glades, near streams. Reported in a few northern Ozark Region counties, also Polk County. June-October.

C   SMOOTH BUR MARIGOLD   *Bidens laevis*

This species has yellow rays and slightly darker, yellow disk flowers. The large flower heads are up to 2 inches (5 cm) wide. The stems are reddish, reclining or upright, and up to 5 feet (1.5 meters) tall. The leaves are smooth, opposite, pointed, slender, and slightly toothed. Seeds of *Bidens* species are eaten by game birds. Aquatic to semiaquatic, often growing with Water-pennywort (*Hydrocotyle*) and other such species. Reported from only Pulaski, Crittenden and Phillips counties at this time. August-November.

   B. cernua, Nodding Bur Marigold, sometimes considered as the same species as *B. laevis,* has flowers that nod with age and few to no rays. Occurrence is scattered over the state in a limited number of counties. July-October.

D   DOLL'S DAISY   *Boltonia diffusa*

The scattered flower heads with white rays and yellow disk flowers are about $^1/_2$ inch (13 mm) wide. The bracts are needlelike. The stems are widely branching and so slender that the flowers often appear to be suspended in air. Other *Boltonia* species have heavier stems and more numerous flowers. Roadsides, woodland edges and openings, low areas. Statewide, but less frequent in northern counties. July-September.

A

B

C

D

A   INDIAN PLANTAIN   ** Cacalia tuberosa*

White to yellowish- white, tubular flower heads are spread flatly across the top of the plant. The top part of the plant has a skeletonlike appearance. The stem leaves are alternate. There is a whorl of large leaves at the base of the plant. These have lengthwise ribs and long petioles. The plants reach 5 feet (1.5 meters) in height. Old fields, slopes, prairies, glades. Widely scattered throughout the state.. June-September.

B   MUSK THISTLE, NODDING THISTLE   *Carduus nutans*

Large, spherical flower heads up to $2^1/_2$ inches (6.3 cm) in diameter are solitary on the long stalks and are usually in a nodding position. There are reflexed purple bracts below the heads. The leaves are up to 10 inches (25 cm) long, sharply lobed and spiny. The plants are up to 5 feet (1.5 meters) tall with sharp, spiny wings along the stems. Native of Europe. Idle or disturbed ground, old fields. A limited number of northern counties, also Lafayette County. June-October.

C   CORNFLOWER, BACHELOR'S BUTTON   *Centaurea cyanus*

Bright blue, white or pink flower heads. The rays are slender near the center of the head and have notched ends. The slender branching stems and slender leaves are light green in color. This is a cultivated species that often escapes. Native of Europe. Old house places, gardens, roadsides, idle land. More common in central and northeastern counties. May-August. Annual.

   C.americana, American Basket Flower, is a tall native annual with large lavender and white, pom pom flowers up to 5 inches in diameter. It occurs mainly in southwestern counties. See page 270.

D   STAR THISTLE, KNAPWEED   *Centaurea maculosa*

The flower heads are whitish to cream-colored in the center and lavender to rose-purple near the edge. There are no ray flowers. The bracts below the heads are marked with a dark triangular tip. The leaves are deeply cut into slender, fingerlike lobes. The stems are numerous and wiry on plants up to about 4 feet (1.2 meters) tall. Alien. Along roadsides, idle fields, glades. Mainly in Ozark Region counties. June-August.

A

D

B

C

A   OX-EYE DAISY   *Chrysanthemum leucanthemum*

Crisp white ray flowers and a large yellow dome of disk flowers make up the flower heads which are carried at the ends of the long stalks. The heads are about 2 inches (5 cm) wide. The numerous basal leaves are cleft. There are few branches on the upright stalks. Native of Europe. Browsed by deer. Fields, meadows, idle ground, roadsides. Mainly in Ozark and Ouachita Mountain Region counties. May-July.

B   COMMON CHICORY, BLUE SAILORS   *Cichorium intybus*

The bright blue flower heads of ray flowers are sessile on the stems and become whitish with age. The tips of the rays are blunt with 5 sharp pointed teeth, a feature of several other composites. The flowers close at mid-day. The upper stems are wiry with few leaves and grow to about 4 feet (1.2 meters) tall. The basal leaves are somewhat like those of the dandelion in form. The roots are sometimes used as a coffee substitute or additive. Native of Europe. Idle land, roadsides. Northern counties. May-October.

C   PURPLE THISTLE   *Cirsium carolinianum*

The bright reddish-purple flower heads have central involucral bracts tipped with spines. Long, bare peduncles. The tall slender plants are up to 7 feet (2.1 meters) high with straight stems having few leaves. The lower leaves are pinnately lobed and downy on the under side. The upper stalks have bracts tipped with spines. Dry soils, open woods, roadsides. Mainly in central counties. May-July.

D   FIELD THISTLE   *Cirsium discolor*

The lavender to slightly pinkish, rarely white, flower head is up to 2 inches (5 cm) long with pointed leaves that curl up around its base. There are long hairs or bristles at the tips of the bracts. The leaves are downy and whitish underneath with large, sharp, spiny lobes. The plants may grow to 8 feet (2.4 meters) high. Some species of thistle furnish seeds that are used by quail for food. Idle land, roadsides, railroads, open woodlands. Recorded in counties across the central part of the state from east to west and in northeastern counties. July-October.

C. altissimum, Tall Thistle, is very similar with less deeply lobed leaves. It occurs nearly statewide. *C. vulgare*, Bull Thistle, has a long, yellow-tipped spine from each of the bracts of the flower head. It is found mainly in northern counties.

A

B

C

D

A   YELLOW THISTLE   *Cirsium horridulum*

The large, pale yellow or pale purplish flower heads are without rays and are about 2 inches (5 cm) wide. Spiny leaves that resemble bracts surround the heads. The leaves are large and spiny, sharply lobed, toothed, and clasp the stems. The stalks are heavy, sometimes branched and grow to 5 feet (1.5 meters) tall. Sandy or rocky open areas, fields, roadsides and railroads. Most often found in the southern counties. May-August.

B   LANCE-LEAVED COREOPSIS   *Coreopsis lanceolata*

Large, yellow, flat flower heads with toothed ray flower ends are up to 2½ inches (6.3 cm) wide. There are 8 ray flowers. The heads are solitary on the long stalks. The leaves are simple, short-stalked and narrow. The plants are eaten by deer. Roadsides, old fields, prairies, idle land. Nearly statewide, less frequent in the Delta Region. April-June.

C. grandiflora, Tickseed, has pinnately lobed upper leaves that are divided to the midrib. The lower leaves are simple. Nearly statewide.

C   TICKSEED, CALLIOPSIS   *Coreopsis tinctoria*

Easily recognized by the yellow ray flowers with a reddish-brown basal area and disk.Slender stems. Leaves divided into slender segments. Idle land, fields, ditches, roadsides. Nearly statewide, but not reported from some of the extreme northern counties.June-September. Annual.

D   PALE-PURPLE CONEFLOWER   *Echinacea pallida*

The flower heads have varying forms and colors. The rays vary in length and width and may be nearly white, greenish-white or a pale reddish-purple. The plants average 3 feet (1 meter) in height and the lower leaves are long-stalked, parallel- veined, narrowly lanceolate and without teeth. Pinelands, cutover areas, prairies, disturbed soils. Nearly statewide, less frequent in the Delta Region. May-July.

A

B

C

D

A   CONEFLOWER   *Echinacea paradoxa*

The yellow rays are strongly downturned and the disk is dark brown. The flower stalks are sturdy and straight, with solitary terminal flowers, and are smooth or slightly hairy with the hairs lying close to the stalk. The leaves are long and slender or very narrowly lanceolate and basal. This is one of several species in the Sunflower Family with this coloring or form that are referred to as "Coneflower." Various coneflowers are preferred deer food plants during the growing season. Limestone slopes and glades. Reported from Baxter, Boone and Stone counties only. May-June.

B   PURPLE CONEFLOWER   *Echinacea purpurea*

The rays in this species are shorter, broader and more purple or reddish than those of Pale-purple Coneflower. In full bloom the disk is orange. The leaves are long-stalked, lanceolate and toothed. Woodland edges and openings, idle land, roadsides. Mainly in the northern two-thirds of the state west of the Delta Region. June-October.

C   CAROLINA ELEPHANT'S FOOT   *Elephantopus carolinianus*

The small flower heads are light shades of violet, lavender or nearly white with only a few florets. The 3 triangular bracts around the head are distinctive in this genus. There are only a few small stem leaves. The larger, lower leaves are long-stalked and oval. The basal leaves usually are absent at time of bloom. The plants average 2 feet (60 cm) tall. Open areas in woodlands, edges of old fields, glades. Shade tolerant. Statewide. July-October.

D   ELEPHANT'S FOOT   *Elephantopus tomentosus*

This species is similar to the above, hut has large, oval or spatulate basal leaves that lie flat on the ground. The flowers are usually darker in color and less spreading. There are more florets in the heads. Central and southern counties. July-September.

A

B

C

D

Erigeron species are widespread, very common and produce an abundance of blossoms. Several of the species are similar. The fruits are eaten by quail.

A DAISY FLEABANE   *Erigeron annuus*

White to light pink ray flowers and a central yellow disk make up the flower heads which are numerous at the tips of the stems, especially in the top part of the plants. The flower heads are about ¹/₂ inch (13mm) wide with relatively short rays that are very narrow. This species has fewer ray flowers than Philadelphia Fleabane. The stem leaves are not clasping. The main leaves are toothed, have hairy edges and are lanceolate. The hairy stems are firm. *Erigeron* species provide food for deer. Idle lands, fields roadsides. Statewide. May-September.

  E. strigosus has linear leaves without teeth. Statewide.

B TALL THOROUGHWORT   *Eupatorium altissimum*

The small white or off-white flower heads are very numerous on the branching stems. The leaves are opposite, sessile, toothed and narrow. The veins from the base of the leaf are not noticibly attached to the midrib. These plants often are 6-7 feet (1.8-2.1 meters) tall. Nearly any type of dry, open area. Mainly recorded in the Ozark and Ouachita Mountain regions. August-October.

C MIST FLOWER, AGERATUM   *Eupatorium coelestinum*

"Misty" or fuzzy groups of flowerheads and the pinkish-violet color are trademarks of this species. The stems are purplish with opposite, toothed leaves that are light green. There are underground runners. Moist areas near streams, roadside ditches, river banks, near takes. Statewide. August-October.

D JOE-PYE WEED   *Eupatorium fistulosum*

The large rounded groups of pale, pinkish-purplish flowers are distinctive. The stems are purplish and hollow. The large pointed leaves are in whorls of 4-7 on tall stalks which reach 8 feet (2.4 meters) or more in height on favorable sites. Damp soils, woodland edges or openings, slopes, along streams. More frequent in northcentral and southwestern counties. July-September.

  E. purpureum, Green-stemmed Joe-Pye Weed, has stems purplish only at the nodes and not hollow. Northern half of the state.

A

B

C

D

A   BONESET   *Eupatorium incarnatum*

This species is somewhat similar to Mist Flower with fewer flowers per head and is a more upright plant with green stems. This species does not produce underground runners. Low fields or open woods, bottom of slopes or bluffs. Widespread in northern counties. Less common in southern counties. August-October.

B   BONESET   *Eupatorium perfoliatum*

Dense groups of small, white flower heads are in clusters, mainly in the top part of the plants. This picture is of a young plant. This species can be recognized by the long, wavy, pointed, opposite leaves that unite around the stem (perfoliate). The plants are 3-5 feet (1-1.5 meters) tall. Browsed by deer. Moist or dry areas, along streams, low open woods, roadside ditches. Nearly statewide but not recorded in some of the northern Ozark Region counties and eastern Delta Region counties. July-October.

   E. rotundifolium, False-horehound, has similar type flowers but the leaves are opposite, sessile, often upturned, and nearly round with evenly spaced teeth. Its range includes the central and southern counties. *E. serotinum*, Late Boneset, has narrow, lanceolate leaves on long petioles and occurs statewide.

C   WHITE SNAKEROOT   *Eupatorhun rugosum*

Pure white. somewhat fuzzv flowers radiate outward from the stalk. There are 15-25 florets in each tuft. The leaves are most often heart-shaped with the bases only slightly indented. The petioles are slender. Plants are up to 3 feet (1 meter) high. Usually in woodlands, often in shaded areas along streams, low ground, slopes. Statewide, fewer records from Delta Region counties. July-October.

D   INDIAN BLANKET, FIRE-WHEELS   *Gaillardia pulchella*

These flower heads are easily recognized by the rays usually having reddish-purple bases and white, pink or yellow tips. The disks are a dark purple. The flower heads are up to 2 inches (5 cm) wide. The leaves are variable on plants up to 2 feet (60 cm) high. Sandy soils, fields, prairies. Mainly limited to the southwestern part of the state. April-November.

   G. aestivalis, usually has yellow disk and ray flowers. The ray flowers are very narrow at the base and the stem leaves are small and oblong. This species is more widespread than the above, occurring in a number of southern counties. July-October.

A

B

C

D

A SWEET EVERLASTING, RABBIT TOBACCO   *Gnaphalium obtusifolium*

There are no ray flowers. The disk flowers are whitish or grayish-white and have a pulpy appearance. The grayish-green leaves persist on the plants for long periods finally turning a lead-gray color. The stems and leaves are covered with downy hairs. The plants are 1-2 feet (30-60 cm) high with numerous slender leaves which furnish food for deer and wild turkey. Dry sites. Statewide. August-October.

    G. purpureum, Purple Cudweed, has flowers similar in form to those of Sweet Everlasting but are reddish-purple, especially in early stages. It is a much smaller plant. The leaves are broader and spatulate. Statewide. Blooms during March-June.

B GUM PLANT   *Grindelia lanceolata*

The ray and disk flowers are yellow with the rays slender and upturned forming a cup-shaped flower head. There are numerous gummy bracts below the head that are of different lengths, creating a ragged appearance. The stems are reddish with lanceolate, upturned leaves that have whitish midribs. The teeth of the leaves are pointed or tipped with bristles. Glades, idle land, roadsides. The Ozark Region, some southern counties. August-October.

C BITTERWEED   *Helenium amarum*

Yellow rays and disks. The flower heads are about ³/₄ inch (18 mm) in diameter. This species can be identified by the numerous, stringlike leaves and the strong, bitter odor and taste which causes livestock to pass it by for better tasting forage. An annual that seldom reaches 2 feet (60 cm) in height. Dry, poor soils of pastures, fields, roadsides. Widespread over the entire state. June-November.

    H. autumnale, Sneezeweed, has larger yellow flowers with downturned rays and lanceolate leaves that are winged onto the stems on tall plants up to 5 feet (1.5 meters) high. Mainly found in the Ozark Region, also in a few southern counties. Along streams, damp soils. A perennial. August- November.

D SNEEZEWEED   *Helenium campestre*

The flower heads have brown disks and down-turned yellow rays. The pappus (compares to the calyx of other flowers) has blunt, toothlike scales. The plants are 2-2 ¹/₂ feet (60-75 cm) tall with very narrow stem leaves. Dry, open woodlands, idle land. Recorded in many of the central and eastern counties. April-June.

    H. flextiosum is similar and is much more widespread. The flowers bloom later and are smaller with more of an orange-yellow in the rays. The rays are at more of a right angle to the stems and the pappus scales are pointed. Grows in moist areas.

A

B

C

D

A   COMMON SUNFLOWER   *Helianthus annuus*

This is the large-flowered species from which cultivated forms have been developed. The flower head may be 3-5 inches (7.5-12.5 cm) in diameter. The stems reach to 9 feet (2.7 meters) in height with very large leaves that are lanceolate to nearly heart-shaped on long petioles. The seeds are eaten by game birds. Idle land, dry open areas, levees, railroads, roadsides. Found mainly in the northern half of the state. May-November.

B   WOODLAND SUNFLOWER   *Helianthus divaricatus*

This species has large flower heads with yellow rays and a darker yellow disk. The stems below the flowers are glabrous. The veins or nerves of the leaf join the midrib at the base. The leaves are opposite, narrowly lanceolate, and hairy underneath, somewhat rough above. Leaves sessile or nearly so. The plants are about 6 feet (1.8 meters) tall when fully grown. Sunflower plants are eaten by deer during the growing season. Open woods, fields, disturbed soils. Statewide, including Crowley's Ridge, less frequent in the Delta Region. July-October.

H.hirsutus, Stiff-haired Sunflower, has stems with stiff hairs. This species often grows in shady woodlands. *H. microcephalus* has more numerous small flowers 1 inch (2.5 cm) wide and smooth stems. It occurs in only a few northeastern counties and on Crowley's Ridge. *H. grossiserratus,* Sawtooth Sunflower, has smooth stems, sawtooth edged leaves which are long, pointed and drooping. The plants grow to 12 feet (3.6 meters) in height. Scattered occurrence. July-October. *Helianthus tuberosus*, Jerusalem Artichoke, is a tall, branching plant with a hairy stalk and irregular-shaped potatolike tubers that are edible. The flowers are much like those of Woodland Sunflower and up to 3 inches (7.5 cm) across. The leaves are lanceolate, hairy on top, downy underneath with coarse teeth, up to 8 inches (20 cm) long. Sometimes cultivated for the tubers. Mainly in central and northern counties and on Crowley's Ridge, Clark County.

C   ASHY SUNFLOWER, HAIRY SUNFLOWER   *Helianthus mollis*

The large flower heads are often well over 2 inches (5 cm) in diameter. The distinguishing features of this species are the upturned, heart-shaped leaves covered with whitish hairs, and the stems, also hairy and erect, with both leaves and flowers well spaced along them. On shorter plants the leaves may be closely spaced. Often occurs in thick stands. Dry soils, openings in woods. Scattered over most of the state. July-September.

D   GOLDEN ASTER   *Heterotheca pilosa*

The small-sized flowers are a bright golden-yellow. Technical characteristics are used to distinguish species in this genus. This species has an inner pappus (calyx) of 20 bristles and an outer pappus of scales. The plants are annuals that are loosely rooted in the ground with stem leaves having a wide, sessile base. Also known as *Chrysopsis pilosa*. Dry or sandy soils, fields, cutovers, openings. Statewide. June-October.

A

B

C

D

A   HAWKWEED   *Hieracium longipilum*

This species is the largest of the genus in Arkansas, having a raceme of flowers 2 feet (60 cm) in length on large specimens. The plants grow to 6 feet (1.8 meters) tall with long hairs on the leaves and lower stems. The leaves are not lobed in the hawkweeds and the flowers are on long stalks. In some other species in this genus the flowers are in panicles. Dry soils, wooded areas, prairies, thin soils. Ozark Region counties, Polk County. July-September.

H. gronovii, Hawkweed, occurs statewide and is a smaller species with flowers in a narrow panicle. There are short hairs on the toothless leaves.

B   OLD PLAINSMAN   *Hymenopappus scabiosaeus*

The whitish, globular flower heads are on slender, branching pedicels and are about $^3/_4$ of an inch (18 mm) in diameter. There are disk flowers only. The leaves are finely divided into slender segments creating a feathery appearance. The plants grow to 5 feet (1.5 meters) high and may be somewhat reclining. Sandy soils, limestone soils. A few southwestern countries, also Benton, Carroll and Washington counties. May-July.

C   WOOLLY-WHITE   *Hymenopappus artemisaefolius*

There are disk flowers only in this species that are white to pink in color in rounded flower heads $^1/_2$ to $^3/_4$ inch (13-18 mm) in diameter. The bracts below the heads are large and white. The heads are on stems that branch at right angles. The plant has a taproot and leaves up to 3 inches (7.5 cm) long with pointed lobes. The upright, single stalks grow up to 5 feet (1.5 meters) tall. Limestone soil, sandy soils, ledges, glades, open ground. Miller, Nevada and Ouachita counties. April-June.

D   POTATO DANDELION   *Krigia dandelion*

The yellow to orange-yellow flower heads are up to $1^1/_2$ inches (3.8 cm) in diameter and have the typical 5-pointed tip on the ray flowers that is characteristic of this and related species of dandelions, false dandelions, dwarf dandelions, cat's ears (*Hypochoeris*), etc. Ray flowers only. The flower stalks are without leaves and there is a small tuber up to 1 inch (2.5 cm) in diameter just under the ground. The leaves are in a basal rosette and are long and slender. Prairies, glades, pinelands, sandy areas, lawns, fields, edges of woods. Statewide. April-June.

A

B

C

D

A FLORIDA LETTUCE   *Latuca floridana*

Small, whitish or bluish flower heads are scattered over a spreading, branching inflorescence (panicle). There are ray flowers only. The smooth leaves are 1 foot (30 cm) in length on the lower part of the tall straight stalks and resemble those of the dandelion in shape. Plants are often 7 feet (2.1 meters) high. A preferred deer food plant. Roadsides, clearings, open woods, old fields. Over most of the state. Few recorded locations in the West Gulf Coastal Plain Region or in the Delta Region except for Crowley's Ridge. August-October.

    L. canadensis, Wild Lettuce, is very similar with yellow ray flowers and occurs statewide. The margins of the leaves are without teeth or prickles. *L. serriola* is a yellow flowered species with prickly dandelion shaped leaves that occurs over most of the state.

    Liatris is a genus of 7-8 species in Arkansas. All of these are very showy with disk flowers only that are lavender to rose-purple. The bracts below the flowers are used as an aid in identification.

B ROUGH BLAZING STAR   *Liatris aspera*

The flower head is very short-stalked or sessile. The buds, which somewhat resemble small cabbages, may remain unopened for long periods. The bracts angle outward and are rounded. Rocky or sandy soils, open areas, cut-overs. Statewide. July-October.

C BLAZING STAR, GAYFEATHER   *Liatris elegans*

The disk flowers in this species have a corolla of wider petals than in other Arkansas species of *Liatris*. The interiors of the flowers are white, with white protruding stamens. Sandy or rocky soils in open areas. Mainly in southwestern counties and northward to Conway, Johnson and Pope counties. August-October.

D BUTTON SNAKEROOT, PRAIRIE GAYFEATHER   *Liatris pycnostachya*

The flower heads are small, crowded and usually a deeper color than in other *Liatris* species. The pointed bracts are recurved. A hairy plant. Prairies, roadsides, cutover pinelands, railroads. Statewide. Last of May-September. Arkansas' earliest *Liatris*.

A

C

B

D

A SCALY BLAZING STAR   *Liatris squarrosa*

A small species with scaly, pointed bracts that extend three-fourths of the way up the flower head. The plants are slender with very slender leaves and are sometimes reclining. Rocky or sandy soils, limestone soils. In all of the regions of the state but somewhat scattered. July-September.

B PALAFOXIA   *Palafoxia callosa*

The flowerheads are pinkish to rose-pink, about $^3/_4$ inch (18 mm) in diameter and have few flowers per head, giving a ragged appearance. The leaves and stems are very slender. The plants are short, seldom exceeding 18 inches (45 cm) in height and have the appearance of a slender clover species. Rocky or limestone glades, sandy or gravelly land, along streams, road shoulders. Northern Ozark Region counties. August-October.

C AMERICAN FEVERFEW, WILD QUININE   *Parthenium integrifolium*

There are white ray and disk flowers. The short disk flowers are numerous and closely grouped, giving the flower head a pulpy appearance. There are only 5 small ray flowers. The leaves are large, thick and toothed on plants up to 3 feet (1 meter) tall. Prairies, glades, rocky areas, woodland edges. Statewide. May-August.

D CAMPHORWEED   **Pluchea purpurascens*

The pinkish-purple, rounded groups of flower heads are at the ends of the stems. There are no ray flowers. The plants are sticky and smell of camphor. The leaves are oval, alternate, lightly toothed and short-stalked or sessile. Idle land, sometimes in disturbed land. Scattered in southern counties. August-November.

   P. camphorata, Stinkweed, has white flowers and is much more widespread. August-September.

A

B

C

D

A   LEAF-CUP   *Polymnia canadensis*

There are white ray flowers and yellow disk flowers. The ray flowers are lobed at the tips. The flower heads are few and are scattered over the plants. The lower leaves are deep green in color, large and cleft into large, angular, toothed lobes. These plants are up to 5 feet (1.5 meters) tall and much branched. Damp, shady woodlands, ravines, slopes. Reported from about half of the Ozark Region counties and a few Ouachita Mountain Region counties. May-October.

     P. uvedalia, Bear's Foot or Yellow Leaf-cup, resembles the above species, vegetatively, but has larger, yellow flower heads and is more widely distributed over the state. July-September.

B   RATTLESNAKE ROOT   *Prenanthes altissima*

The flowers usually have 5 bracts and are a creamy-white color near the tips. They hang, belllike, from the upper branches. The leaves are of various shapes but often are heart-shaped as shown. The plants are up to 6 feet (1.8 meters) in height. Damp woods. Mainly in the Ozark and Ouachita Mountain regions. July-September.

C   FALSE DANDELION   *Pyrrhopappus carolinianus*

The flower heads resemble those of the common dandelion and also have all ray flowers but these are a light yellow color, larger, and with a ring of small, dark markings near the center of the head. Each flower lasts only a day or two and usually closes by noon. The early basal leaves are lobed somewhat like those of the common dandelion, but at blooming time they may be absent or consist of slender-bladed, even-edged leaves that taper to a point. There are few stem leaves. Idle land, roadsides, sandy or rocky open areas, often on poor soil. Statewide. May-October.

D   LONG-HEADED CONEFLOWER, MEXICAN HAT   *Ratibida columnaris*

The drooping ray flowers are broad and usually reddish-brown at the base or nearly to the tip of the ray. The receptable on which the disk flowers is carried is long and rounded. The entire flower head is up to 2 inches (5 cm) long. The leaves are mainly confined to the lower half of the plant and have slender segments. Plants average 2 feet (60 cm) high. Prairies, open areas, pinelands. Reported from widely scattered locations. June-October.

A

B

C

D

A   GRAY-HEAD CONEFLOWER, DROOPING CONEFLOWER   *Ratibida pinnata*

The drooping rays and large gray disks are aids in recognizing this species. The leaves are lobed into several slender segments and have small whitish hairs. The stems are hairy. The plants grow to 5 feet (1.5 meters) high and are often abundant along roadsides in extreme northern counties. Idle land, fields, roadsides, open areas. Northern part of the Ozark Region, also Clark and Hempstead counties. June-September.

B   LARGE CONEFLOWER   *Rudbeckia grandiflora*

The large flower heads have yellow rays and large brown disks. The rays are nearly 3 inches (7.5 cm) long and are usually drooping. The disk becomes cone-shaped and nearly 1 inch (2.5 cm) long. The lobes of the disk flowers are drooping. Tall, slender stalks. The leaves are upright, smaller up the stalk and lanceolate to oblong. Plants often are in dense stands. Open, dry areas, especially prairies and undisturbed ground. Nearly statewide. July-August.

C   BLACK-EYED SUSAN   *Rudbeckia hirta*

The yellow rays and dark brown disk flowers are in large flower heads about 2$\frac{1}{2}$ inches (7.5 cm) in diameter. There is one head on each slender, hairy stem. The leaves are hairy, long-oval in shape with the lower ones stalked. The plants are 2-3 feet (60-90 cm) tall. This species is variable. *Rudbeckia* species furnish browse for deer. Idle land, old fields, eroded land, roadsides, railroads. Statewide. May-October.

   R. triloba, Brown-eyed Susan, is similar but with shorter and fewer rays and with some lower leaves 3-lobed, up to 6 feet (1-1.8 meters) tall and branching. Usually found along streams. Northwestern half of the state. June-October. *R. laciniata* has long yellow ray flowers that angle downward and a greenish-yellow disk which has added another common name: Green-headed Coneflower. The leaves are cut almost to the midrib into 3-5 lobes. The plants are usually 3-6 feet (1-1.8 meters) tall but may grow to 9 feet (2.7 meters) high on favorable sites. Moist ground, woodland edges, open slopes, near streams. Ozark Region counties and a few Ouachita Mountain Region counties. July-September.

D   GOLDEN RAGWORT, SQUAW-WEED   *Senecio aureus*

The flower heads are golden yellow. The stems are reddish-brown with long-stemmed, heart-shaped basal leaves and pinnately divided upper leaves. The plants are up to 3 feet (1 meter) or more in height. Along streams, low ground, wet woodlands, near swamps or low meadows. Scattered in a few Ozark and Ouachita Mountain Region counties. April-June.

A

D

B

C

A BUTTERWEED, GROUNDSEL *Senecio glabellus*

The flower heads are a rich, golden-yellow and are closely grouped at the tips of the stems. Individual flower heads are about 1 inch (2.5 cm) in diameter. There is a basal rosette of leaves and alternate stem leaves that are divided into rounded, pinnately arranged lobes. The terminal lobe is larger. The edges of the lobes are toothed and the entire plant is glabrous with hollow stems up to 3 feet (1 meter) tall. Eaten by deer. Alluvial soils in woods, fields, roadsides, on both open and shaded sites. Over much of the state except for some of the counties in the western and northern sections. March-May.

B COMPASS PLANT *Silphium laciniatum*

The flower heads are short-stemmed and grow on the upper part of the stalk facing in all directions. The sharp-pointed bracts are recurved. The lower, alternate leaves are very long, 1-1½ feet (30-45 cm), and deeply cut into long pinnate lobes with 1-3 large teeth on each. The upper stems secrete a gummy sap. The tall slender plants are usually unbranched and are 4-10 feet (1.2-3 meters) tall. Prairies, open areas, roadsides. Scattered in central and northcentral counties, Grand Prairie. July-September.

S. integrifolium, Rosin-weed, is a tall plant with more separated rays. The paired leaves are without stalks or teeth. The plants often ooze a sticky sap. Statewide except for a few Ozark Region counties.

C CUP PLANT *Silphium perfoliatum*

There are 20-30 yellow rays and darker yellow disks. Numerous flower heads occur on the larger plants. The opposite leaves encircle the square stem forming a cup that may hold water after rains. The leaves are lanceolate in outline with irregular margins and up to 1 foot (30 cm) long. The upper stems are usually purplish in color and up to 8 feet (2.4 meters) high. Near rivers and streams, valleys, roadsides. Mainly in northern counties and a few central counties. July-September.

D PRAIRIE DOCK *Silphium terebinthinaceum*

An easily recognized species, even when not in bloom, because of the very large, wide, spade-shaped leaves. The plants are up to 9 feet (2.7 meters) tall. The flower heads are numerous on older plants. Usually on limestone soils, ledges, road banks, glades, prairies. Northern Ozark Region counties. July-October.

A

B

C

D

Solidago is a very large genus which includes the goldenrods. Over 20 species have been collected within the state. They vary in form from tall spreading plants to slender wandlike or flat-topped species. Deer eat the leaves of some of the species. Turkeys eat the seeds.

A   BLUE-STEM GOLDENROD, WREATH GOLDENROD   *Solidago caesia*

In this species the flower heads have 3-5 rays and are in tufts spaced along the stem in the axils of the leaves. The leaves are long, slender and slightly toothed. The stems are often arching or nearly reclining, purplish in color with a slight glaucous coating, and up to 3 feet (1 meter) long. Woodlands, shady areas and edges. Scattered over the state. July-October.

B   CANADA GOLDENROD   *Solidago canadensis*

Young plants have pyramid-shaped inflorescences which later spread into long arching stems with yellow plumes of flowers with 9-15 rays per flower head. The individual heads are only $1/8$ inch (3 mm) long. The leaves are numerous, slender, and pointed, with sharp teeth. The upper and lower leaf surfaces have numerous hairs. This is one of the more common species of goldenrod. Woodland openings, roadsides, fields. Nearly statewide, less common in western and northwestern counties. July-September.

C   GOLDENROD   *Solidago petiolaris*

The flower heads are large and separated in this species. They are grouped fairly closely to the main stem of the plant. The leaves are large, lanceolate and slightly toothed becoming smaller toward the top of the plant. Open areas, glades, rocky slopes. Over most of the western two-thirds of the state. August-October.

S. flexicaulis, Broadleaf Goldenrod, can be recognized by the wide leaves and the tufts of flower heads in the leaf axils. The main stem is a zig-zag shape and angled. Open and shaded woodlands. Occurs in only a few scattered Ozark Region counties, Lee County. July-October.

D   COMMON DANDELION   *Taraxicum officinale*

The bright yellow flowers (all rays) and irregular, sharp-lobed leaves are familiar to most people. This is the common lawnweed species. Native of Europe. The plants furnish food for deer. Lawns, curbs, vacant lots, road shoulders, open areas. Statewide. March-October, often in other months.

Sonchus asper, Spiney-leaved Sow Thistle, has small yellow, thistle-shaped flower heads and curling, spiney leaves with bases circling the stems. It is up to 5 feet (1.5 meters) tall and occurs over most of the state. The blooming period is June-September.

A

B

C

D

A GOAT'S BEARD   *Tragopogon dubius*

A yellow flower head with long, slender bracts that resemble sepals and extend past the rays. The flowers usually close by noon. The large feathery seed heads are about 3 inches (7.5 cm) in diameter. Long, slender leaves clasp the stems which are up to 2½ feet (75 cm) tall. Native of Europe. Roadsides, glades, open woods, railroads. Scattered northern counties. May-July.

B YELLOW IRONWEED   *Verbesina alternifolia*

The flower heads have up to 8 drooping rays that are broad and bright yellow. The spherical groups of disk flowers are green to yellow depending upon the age. The leaves are alternate, lanceolate, finely toothed and have leaf tissue extending along the stalks. The plants grow to 8 feet (2.4 meters) tall. Along rivers, and streams, other low, wet areas. More common in the northern half of the state. August-October.

C WINGSTEM   *Verbesina helianthoides*

The rays are irregular but not drooping and more numerous (8-15) than in the above species. The stems are winged and the leaves are alternate. The plants grow to about 4 feet (1.2 meters) high. Dry, often rocky soils, open woods, prairies, disturbed areas. Statewide but not common in the Delta Region. May-July.

D WHITE CROWN-BEARD, FROSTWEED   *Verbesina virginica*

There are only 3-5 white rays per flower head and grayish disk flowers. These flowers are very attractive to butterflies and other insects. The winged stalks grow to 7 feet (2.1 meters) tall and form "frost flowers" just above ground level when the first hard freeze forces water out of the stems to form various rounded or curving shapes of ice. The leaves are broadly lanceolate with few teeth. Eaten by deer. Along streams, roadsides, open slopes and valleys. Nearly statewide, less common in southeastern counties. August-October.

A

B

C

D

A VERBESINA   *Verbesina walteri*

May be recognized by the rounded, whitish, flower heads consisting entirely of disk flowers (no rays). These are about ¹/₂ inch (13 mm) in diameter. The leaves are slender in the top part of the plant to more lanceolate below and only slightly toothed. The stems are winged. Wooded hills and slopes. Shady areas. Known only from a few Ouachita Mountain Region counties. August-October.

B ARKANSAS IRONWEED   *Vernonia arkansana*

There are large flower heads of purple to reddish-purple disk flowers and long, curled involucre bracts. The plants are erect to reclining with long, slender, willowlike leaves and grow to about 3 feet (1 meter) high. Ironweeds hybridize to a great extent often making identification of the species very difficult. This species is usually found along streams, on gravel bars, rocky moist slopes, open woods, sometimes prairies or glades. The range coincides closely to the Ozark Region. July-October.

C TALL IRONWEED   *Vernonia gigantea*

The flower heads have 13-30 individual disk flowers. The narrow, purple-tipped bracts are without hairs and are blunt. The pappus is purple. The plants may be 7 feet (2.1 meters) in height with leaves that are slender and lanceolate or elliptic with small straight hairs on the lower surface that are more numerous on the midrib. The leaves are up to 8 inches (20 cm) long. Moist areas. Statewide. July-October.

D LETTERMAN'S IRONWEED   *Vernonia lettermanii*

A relatively short-growing ironweed with numerous needlelike leaves about 3 inches (7.5 cm) long. Rocky or sandy open areas. Southwestern counties, Faulkner County. August-September.

264

A

B

C

D

ADDENDUM
* New Scientific Names

		Old Name	**New Name**
Page	24 -	Alisma plantago-aquatica	Alisma subcordatum
	40 -	Smilacina racemosa	Maianthemum paniculatum
	52 -	Sisyrinchium exile	Sisyrinchium rosulatum
	68 -	Polygonum coccineum	Polygonum amphibium
	72 -	Arenaria patula	Minuaritia patula
	74 -	Lychnis alba	Silene pratensis
	76 -	Nuphar luteum	Nuphar lutea
	78 -	Actaea pachypoda	Actaea alba
	90 -	Cardamine bulbosa	Cardamine rhomboidea
	90 -	Dentaria laciniata	Cardamine concatenata
	92 -	Nasturtium officinale	Rorrippa nasturtium aquaticum
	94 -	Streptanthus maculatus	Streptanthus obtusifolius
		(An Oklahoma species)	(Our plants are this species)
	94 -	Cleome spinosa	Cleome hassleriana
	100 -	Fragaria virginianum	Fragaria virginiana
	102 -	Gillenia stipulatus	Porteranthus stipulatus
	108 -	Baptisia leucantha	Baptisia alba
	108 -	Baptisia leucophea	Baptisia bracteata
	110 -	Cassia fasciculata	Chamaecrista fasciculata
	110 -	Cassia marilandica	Senna marilandica
	110 -	Cassia obtusifolia	Senna obtusifolia
	110 -	Cassia occidentalis	Senna occidentalis
	116 -	Petalostemon candidium	Dalea candida
	116 -	Petalostemon purpureum	Dalea purpurea
	122 -	Vicia dasycarpa	Vicia villosa
	136 -	Hibiscus moscheutos	Hibiscus lasiocarpos
		subsp. lasiocarpos	
	144 -	Viola pensylvanica	Viola pubecsens
	146 -	Opuntia compressa	Opuntia humifusa
	152 -	Oenothera biennis	Oenothera villosa
	154 -	Oenothera missouriensis	Oenothera macrocarpa
	164 -	Gentiana flavida	Gentiana alba
	164 -	Gentiana quinquefolia	Gentianella quinquefolia
	166 -	Swertia caroliniensis	Frasera caroliniensis
	172 -	Convolvulus sepium	Calystegia sepium
	184 -	Verbena bipinnatifida	Glandularia bipinnatifida
	184 -	Verbena canadensis	Glandularia canadensis
	198 -	Aureolaria pedicularia	Aureolaria pectinata
	206 -	Seymeria macrophylla	Dasistoma macrophylla
	216 -	Lonicera flava	Lonicera dioica
	224 -	Antennaria plantaginifolia	Antennaria parlinii
	232 -	Cacalia tuberosa	Cacalia plantaginea
	252 -	Pluchea putpurascens	Pluchea odorata
	254 -	Ratibida columnaris	Ratibida columnifera

Glossary

Alien: From another country. Exotic.

Alluvial: Soil deposited by water.

Alternate: Leaves, located singly at intervals along the stem,

Annual: Plant, living and producing fruit in one growing season.

Anther: That part of the stamen that bears pollen.

Aquatic: Growing in water.

Axil: The space between the petiole and the stem.

Basal: Leaves, at the base of the plant.

Biennial: Plant, living for two growing seasons and producing flowers and fruit the second season.

Bisexual: Having both stamen and pistil in the same flower; a perfect flower.

Blade: The broader part of the leaf between the midrib and the edge.

Bract: A small leaflike structure, usually associated with flowering parts.

Bulb: An underground, fleshy enlargement of stem and leaves as in the onion.

Calyx: All of the sepals or outer parts of the flower.

Capsule: A dry fruit of more than one carpel.

Carpel: A simple seed vessel from one pistil.

Cm (Centimeter):   One hundredth of a meter. 1 inch equals about 2.5 cm.

Clasping: The leaf base partly or entirely surrounding the stem.

Colony: A group of individual plants.

Composites: Refers to species of the Sunflower Family.

Compound: A combination of 2 or more similar parts as in compound leaves.

Corm: An enlarged underground stem that stores food. Bulblike but firm, often covered with thin, scalelike leaves.

Corolla: All of the petals of a flower.

Cultivated: Purposely grown plant.

Dicotyledon: Having two seed leaves as in a bean or pea.

Disk: The central tubular flowers in the flower head of some members of the Sunflower family.

Dissected: Cut into lobes or divisions.

Endemic: A plant native to a restricted area.

Escape: A plant growing wild that was formerly cultivated.

Female: A flower with one or more pistils but no stamens; a pistillate flower.

Fibrous: Having the composition of fibers.

Filament: The stalk of the stamen.

Form: A variance in a species.

Fruit: The structure which contains the seed and is produced by the flower.

Genera: Plural of genus.

Genus: A group of similar plants having the same first name of the binomial system.

Glabrous: Without hairs, smooth.

Gland: An organ that secretes or any similarly shaped organ.

Glaucous: Covered with a powdery substance.

Habitat: The surroundings in which a plant grows.

Head: A dense cluster of flowers.

Herb: A plant without woody tissue that dies after one growing season.

Herbaceous: Having the character of a herb.

Hood: A curved extension of a floral part.

Hybrid: A plant produced by interbreeding of two separate species.

Inflorescence: The flower cluster.

Involucre: A series of bracts at the base of a flower or inflorescence as in the Sunflower Family.

Irregular: A flower of irregularly shaped parts but having bilateral symmetry.

Lanceolate: See page 271.

Leaflet: One of the leaflike segments of a compound leaf.

Linear: See page 271.

Lip: One of the two large divisions of the corolla of some bilaterally symmetrical flowers.

Lobe: A part of a flower or leaf that bulges outward.

Male: A flower with one or more stamens but no pistils; a staminate flower.

Meter: A unit of length in the metric system of 39.31 inches. Contains 100 centimeters (cm) or 1000 millimeters (mm).

Midrib: The primary vein of a leaf, usually the central structure.

Mm (Millimeter):   One thousandth of a meter. 1 inch equals about 25 mm.

Monocotyledon: Having one seed leaf as in a grass or lily seed.

Native: A plant that is natural to an area.

Naturalized: An alien plant that adapts to another habitat.

Node: The location of the stem from which leaves, buds or other structures grow.

Oblong: See page 271.

Opposite: Leaves, located directly across from each other on the stem.

Ovary: The basal enlarged area of the pistil in which seeds develop.

Ovate: See page 271.

Palmate: See page 272.

Panicle: See page 273.

Pappas: A modification of the calyx that consists of hairs, awns, bristles or scales on the flowers and fruits of composites.

Pedicel: The stalk bearing a single flower.

Peduncle: The stalk bearing a flower cluster.

Perfect: A flower having both male and female parts (both stamen and pistil in the same flower.).

Perennial: Living from year to year.

Perfoliate: Leaf blades surrounding the stem of the plant so that the stem appears to pass through the leaf.

Petal: One of the parts of the corolla, usually brightly colored.

Petiole: The stem of a leaf.

Pinnate: See page 272.

Pistil: The female reproductive organ of a plant consisting of stigma, style and ovary.

Pistillate: A flower with one or more pistils but no stamens; a female flower.

Pubescent: Covered with small hairs.

Raceme: An inflorescence, usually elongated, with stalked flowers along the main stem. See page 273.

Ray: The outer flowers in the flower head of some members of the Sunflower Family.

Recurved: Curved away from other structures.

Regular: Symmetrical flowers with parts that are of similar size and shape.

Rhizome: An underground fleshy stem, usually horizontal, from which modified leaves arise at the nodes as in the iris.

Rosette: Leaves, arranged in a circle at the base of the plant.

Sac: A pouch or cavity, especially in a flower part.

Saprophyte: Lives on dead or decaying organic matter.

Sepal: A single part of the calyx or outer group of flower parts.

Sessile: Without a stalk.

Sheath: A structure which surrounds another.

Simple: Single or of one piece.

Spadix: A fleshy stem on which numerous small flowers grow.

Spathe: A large bract around the spadix.

Spatulate: See page 271.

Species: A group of plants differing from each other in only minor characteristics. Indicated by the second name of the binomial system.

Spike: An unbranched inflorescence of stalkless flowers. See page 273.

Spur: A tubular extension, usually of a flower part.

Stalk: Usually refers to the main stem of the plant or inflorescence.

Stamen: The male reproductive organ of a plant, consisting of anther and filament.

Staminate: A flower with one or more stamens but no pistils. A male flower.

Stem: Usually refers to the main stalk or branches of a plant.

Sterile: Does not produce viable fruiting bodies.

Stigma: The top of the pistil that receives the pollen.

Stipules: A pair of structures at the base of the petiole, usually attached to the stem of the plant. May be small and leaflike or modified into tendrils, spines, etc.

Style: A sort of stem between the stigma and ovary of the pistil.

Succulent: Fleshy, juicy and soft.

Symmetrical: Having parts of nearly equal size and shape and radially arranged.

Taproot: A large, elongated root, usually vertical.

Tendril: A usually slender, coiled, elongated organ that attaches to other objects in climbing plants.

Terminal: At the end of.

Trifoliate: Having three leaflets, as in clovers.

Tuber: A compact underground stem storing food, usually horizontal as in the Irish potato.

Umbel: See page 273.

Variety: A variation from the usual species characteristics.

Vein: Strands of vascular tissue as in leaves.

Weed: Any plant growing where it is not wanted or is troublesome to some purpose.

Whorl: Groups of leaves, flowers or stems arranged in a circular pattern.

Wing: A more or less flattened structure alongside another.

Wort: A plant used for some purpose or resembling some other object as in toothwort.

FLY POISON
See page 46

Amianthium muscaetoxicum

YELLOW FLAG
See page 52

Iris pseudacorus

LEATHER FLOWER
See page 80

Clematis viorna

BASKET FLOWER
See page 232

Centaurea americana

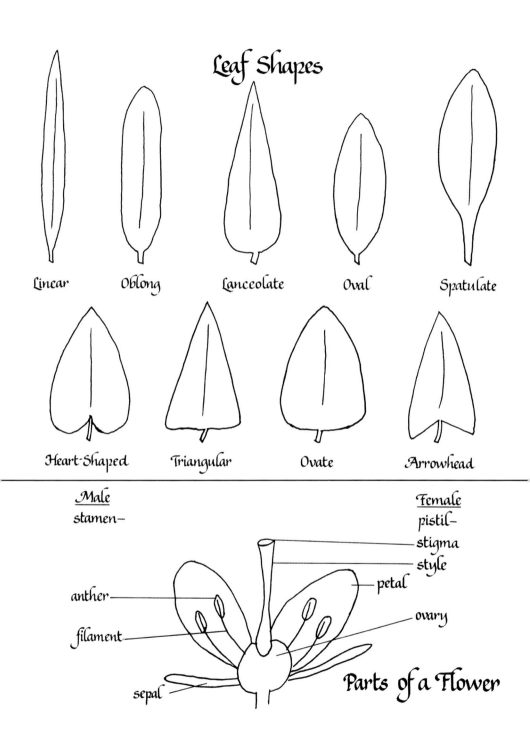

Leaf Shapes

Linear   Oblong   Lanceolate   Oval   Spatulate

Heart-Shaped   Triangular   Ovate   Arrowhead

Male
stamen—

Female
pistil—
stigma
style

petal

anther

ovary

filament

sepal

Parts of a Flower

Simple Leaf

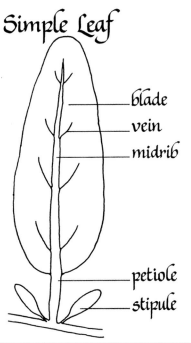

- blade
- vein
- midrib
- petiole
- stipule

Compound Leaves

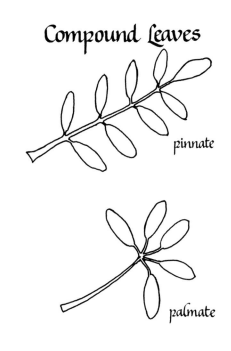

pinnate

palmate

Leaf Positions

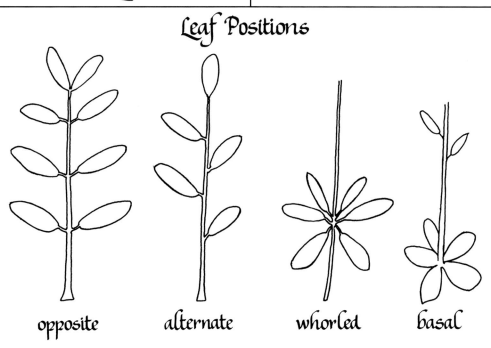

opposite   alternate   whorled   basal

Flower Arrangements

terminal

spike

raceme

panicle

umbel

REFERENCES

Brown, Claire A.
1972, *Wildflowers of Louisiana,* Louisiana State University Press, Baton Rouge.

Denison, Edgar
1978, *Missouri Wildflowers,* Missouri Department of Conservation, Jefferson City.

Donaldson, David, Carl Hunter and T.H. Holder
1951, *Arkansas'Deer Herd,* Arkansas Game and Fish Commission, Little Rock.

Duncan, Wilbur H. and Leonard E. Foote
1975, *Wildflowers of the Southeastern* United States, University of Georgia Press, Athens.

Ettman, James K. and David R. McAdoo
1979, *An Annotated Catalog and Distribution Account of the Kentucky Orchidaceae,* The Kentucky Society of Natural History Charitable Trust, Louisville.

Foster, Steven and James A. Duke
1990, *A Field Guide to Medicinal Plants,* Houghton Mifflin Co., Boston.

Halls, Lowell K. and Thomas H. Ripley
1961, *Deer Browse Plants of Southern Forests,* U.S. Forest Service-South and Southeast,Washington, D.C.

Hewitt, Oliver H., Editor
1967, *The Wild Turkey and Its Management,* The Wildlife Society.

Huey, Edith Lancaster
1977, *Ozark Wild Flowers,* Woods Brothers Agency, Little Rock, Arkansas.

Huey, Edith Lancaster
1978, *Ozark Wild Flowers II,* Woods Brothers Agency, Little Rock, Arkansas.

Huey, Edith Lancaster
1984, *Ozark Wild Flowers III,* Woods Brothers Agency, Little Rock, Arkansas.

Hunter, Carl G.
1989, *Trees, Shrubs, and Vines of Arkansas,* The Ozark Society Foundation, Little Rock, Arkansas.

Hunter, Carl G.
1995, *Autumn Leaves & Winter Berries in Arkansas,* The Ozark Society Foundation, Little Rock, Arkansas.

Johnson, Lady Bird and Carlton B. Lees
1988, *Wildflowers Across America,* Abbeville Press, New York.

Klimas, John E. and Jaynes A. Cunningham
1974, *Wildflowers of Eastern America,* Alfred A. Knopf, Inc., New York.

Linn, Louis C.
1978, *Eastern North America's Wildflowers,* E.P. Dutton, New York.

Martin, Alexander C., Herbert S. Zin, Arnold L. Nelson
1951, *American Wildlife & Plants, A Guide to Wildlife Food Habits,* Dover Publications, Inc., New York.

Murphy, Dean A. and Hewlett S. Crawford
1970, *Wildlife Foods and Understory Vegetation in Missouri National Forests.* Missouri Department of Conservation, Jefferson City.

National Wildflower Research Center
1989, *Wildflower Handbook,* Texas Monthly Press, Austin.

Niering, William A. and Nancy C. Olmstead
1979, *The Audubon Society Field Guide to North American Wildflowers,* Alfred A. Knopf, New York.

Peterson, Roger T. and Margaret McKenny
1968, *A Field Guide to Wildflowers of Northeastern and North-central North America,* Houghton Mifflin Co., Boston.

Phillips, Harry R.
1985, *Growing and Propagating Wildflowers,* University of North Carolina Press, Chapel Hill.

Radford, Albert E., Harry E. Ahles and C. Ritchie Bell
1974, *Manual oj'the Vascular Flora of the Carolinas,* University of North Carolina Press, Chapel Hill.

Reader's Digest
1986, *Magic and Medicine of Plants,* Reader's Digest Association, Pleasantville, New York.

Rickert, Harold W.
1966, *Wildflowers of the United States: The Southeastern States, 2* Volumes, McGraw-Hill Book Co., New York.

Slaughter, Carl R.
1993, *Wild Orchids of Arkansas,* Morrilton.

Smith, Edwin B.
1978, *An Atlas and Annotated List of the Vascular Plants of Arkansas,* University of Arkansas Bookstore, Fayetteville.

Smith, Edwin B.
1994, *Keys to the Flora of Arkansas,* University of Arkansas Press, Fayetteville.

Sperka, Marie
1973, *Growing Wildflowers,* Charles Scribner's Sons, New York.

Stevens, William Chase
1961, *Kansas Wild Flowers,* University of Kansas Press, Lawrence.

Steyermark, J.A.
1963, *Flora of Missouri,* Iowa State University Press, Ames.

Stoddard, Herbert L.
1946, *The Bobwhite Quail,* Charles Scribner's Sons, New York.

Sweeney, James M., C. Richard Wenger and Noel S. Yoho
1981, *Bobwhite Quail Food in Young Arkansas Loblolly Pine Plantations,* University of Arkansas, Fayetteville.

Tatum, Billy Joe
1976, *Wildfoods Cookbook and Field Guide,* Workman Publishing Co., New York.

Timme, S. Lee
1989, *Wildflowers of Mississippi,* University Press of Mississippi, Jackson.

Wade, Ruth Gier
1977, *Arkansas Wildflowers,* White Publishing Co., Paragould.

Wharton, Mary E. and Roger W. Barbour
1971, *A Guide to the Wildflowers and Ferns of Kentucky,* University Press of Kentucky, Lexington.

PHOTOGRAPHERS

Most of the photographs were taken by the author. A special thanks is due the following people who supplied photographs as indicated by the page number and letter.

Campbell, Breck, Little Rock   167C

Cartwright, Mike, Fifty-Six   155C

Clark, Joe and Maxine, Fayetteville   87D, 175D, 243D, 251B

Ettman, Jim, Morrilton   35A, 55B, 57A, 59A, 157C, 161B, 209D

Evans, Herb, Little Rock   155B, 181C, 217B

Ewing,Lana,Mena   37C, 39C, 43A, 71C, 95A, 117B, 163D, 179C, 261B, 265D

Gregory, Edwin, Parkdale   29B, 33C, 47D, 97B, 137D, 147D, 195D, 203B, 219A, 223B, 225B,249D

Hall, Ed, Little Rock   57B, 75D, 131B, 155A, 201B, 211D, 251C, 255B, 270-1

Haller, Karen, Ballwin, Mo.   193D

Heineke, Tom, Memphis, Tenn.   85A

Hicks, Betty, Little Rock   61A

Huey, Edith, Mountain View   101B, 187A, 229B

Johnson, Randy, Roland   47B, 79B, 133C, 237A

Kurz, Don, Jefferson City, Mo.   141D, 161D, 167A

Pelton, John, Benton   39B, 183C, 195A

Poe, Joe Allen, Little Rock   63B, 65B, 67C, 189D, 211A

Shepherd, Bill, Little Rock   53B, 149B, 229D

Slaughter, Carl, Morrilton   57C, 65C, 127C, 253A

Smith, Kenneth, Little Rock   239A

Stern, Howard S., Pine Bluff   89B, 255D

Timme, Steve, Pittsburg, Kansas   65A, 79A, 87B, 137B, 145A, 165B, 179B, 219B, 247A

Index

282

286

287